'Karen Dean and Sam Humphrey ha
bringing the reader closer to an under
in the mind of coaches and helps the r......
experiences from real people in their prospective fields. It's a great book
for anyone wanting to develop both their coaching and personal leadership skills so you can truly be that confident and inspiring person you
know you are.'

> – **Craig Revel Horwood**, from the foreword

'I've been coached and in turn coached others, first in sport and now far
beyond, walking with clients through some of the most challenging personal and business chapters of their lives. I now have a cohort of colleagues
who provide support and challenge in equal measure, but I know my journey in coaching would have been enhanced by a book like this, where
key elements of coaching practice are illustrated with heart-warming
stories, all within a cogent coaching framework, from which we can all
take something – no matter our coaching background or experience.'

> – **John Amaechi** OBE, organisational psychologist,
> Chartered Scientist, *New York Times* best-selling
> author and CEO of APS, a leadership consultancy
> working in Europe and the United States

'Karen and Sam are up to something, inspiring you to dream, learn and
be more of who you are as a coach and leader.'

> – **Steve Radcliffe**, leadership expert and author of the
> UK's top leadership book *Leadership Plain and Simple*

'This highly personal account by two seasoned coaches takes you behind
the scenes. Packed with numerous real examples from their professional
practice Karen Dean and Sam Humphrey candidly describe their ups and
downs and the challenges they have faced as coaches. By far the most
important take away I believe is that through it all they have continued
learning – and so will you.'

> – **Ian McDermott**, founder of International Teaching Seminars,
> creator of 'Mastering the Coach Approach' and author of
> *The NLP Coach, Your Inner Coach* and *The Coaching Bible*

'What a rare treat . . . to walk alongside two pioneer coaches as they navigate the challenges, set-backs and triumphs emblematic of the journey
from beginner to master coach. Their journey is even more admirable

when we consider that they began their careers before most of the major professional coaching bodies were even born or were in their infancies. Through humility, humour and grace, their stories illuminate how coaching holds the promise of tremendous value, is not for the faint of heart, cannot be done by just anyone, and requires highly specialized knowledge, skills and abilities on the part of the coach. This book shows us how courage, critical reflection, appropriate education and training and a fierce commitment to an ongoing learning journey are imperatives for any coach wishing to offer credible personal or business coaching services in the marketplace today.'

— **Wendy Johnson**, founder, President/CEO of the Worldwide Association of Business Coaches (WABC)

Coaching Stories

Being a coach is a deeply rewarding profession, but even the best coaches encounter moments of uncertainty and doubt. In *Coaching Stories: Flowing and Falling of Being a Coach*, Karen Dean and Sam Humphrey intimately share their varied experiences as executive coaches in 48 stories – some where they were flowing and glorious, and others where they were falling and ashamed.

Dean and Humphrey guide the reader through the journey from a novice to a master coach by exploring twelve distinct themes, underpinned by the four parts of Dean's 'Exceptional Achievement' framework: setting out, doing, integrating and being. Each chapter focuses on a different theme, presenting specific examples and stories from the authors' work and reflecting on their learning and development at each point. Dean and Humphrey expertly assess topics, including confidence, talent, purpose and fulfilment, by examining times where they performed effectively as well as those where they fell short. In each case they consider what they wish they had asked or known about in advance, and each story provides an insightful look at what being a coach is really like. Practical and accessible, the book concludes with a section on further reading and study, explaining relevant theories, models and frameworks.

Coaching Stories: Flowing and Falling of Being a Coach will be a compassionate and pragmatic companion for coaches of all kinds, both in practice and in training. It will also be a valuable guide for other professionals seeking development, including internal coaches, managers in a coaching role, HR and L&D professionals, and will be a useful text for academics and students of coaching and coaching psychology.

Dean and Humphrey are award-winning authors and have written a number of articles for leading coaching publications.

Karen Dean is a Master Certified Coach accredited by the International Coach Federation, which places her in the top one per cent of ICF-credentialed coaches in the UK and a coach supervisor. She works with senior clients across 22 sectors, worldwide.

Sam Humphrey is an accredited coach, supervisor, researcher and author. She is one of the founding members of the editorial board for the *Coaching at Work* magazine and was one of the first 25 people to complete a Masters in Coaching. She is the former Global Head of Coaching for Unilever and has more than two decades' professional coaching experience.

Coaching Stories

Flowing and Falling of Being a Coach

Karen Dean and
Sam Humphrey

Routledge
Taylor & Francis Group

LONDON AND NEW YORK

First published 2019
by Routledge
2 Park Square, Milton Park, Abingdon, Oxon OX14 4RN

and by Routledge
52 Vanderbilt Avenue, New York, NY 10017

Routledge is an imprint of the Taylor & Francis Group, an informa business

British Library Cataloguing-in-Publication Data
A catalogue record for this book is available from the British Library

Library of Congress Cataloging-in-Publication Data
Names: Dean, Karen, 1957- author. | Humphrey, Sam, 1967- author.
Title: Coaching stories : flowing and falling of being a coach / Karen
    Dean and Sam Humphrey.
Description: Abingdon, Oxon ; New York, NY : Routledge, 2019. |
    Includes bibliographical references and index.
Identifiers: LCCN 2018049135 (print) | LCCN 2018050727 (ebook)
    | ISBN 9780429428227 (Master eBook) | ISBN 9780429766336
    (Mobipocket) | ISBN 9780429766350 (Abode Reader) | ISBN
    9781138370098 (hardback) | ISBN 9781138370104 (pbk.)
Subjects: LCSH: Personal coaching. | Executive coaching.
Classification: LCC BF637.P36 (ebook) | LCC BF637.P36 D43 2019
    (print) | DDC 158.3—dc23
LC record available at https://lccn.loc.gov/2018049135

ISBN: 978-1-138-37009-8 (hbk)
ISBN: 978-1-138-37010-4 (pbk)
ISBN: 978-0-429-42822-7 (ebk)

Typeset in Times New Roman
by Swales & Willis Ltd, Exeter, Devon, UK

Printed and bound in Great Britain by
TJ International Ltd, Padstow, Cornwall

My husband, Charlie, who is a source of fun, joy and love, every day. Tom and Matt, my fine sons, who are making your differences in life. *Karen*

For Teddy, Lily and James – my first, my last, my everything. *Sam*

Contents

Acknowledgements

There are a significant number of people who have contributed directly and indirectly to this book and whose encouragement, love and belief in us we would like to acknowledge.

First, we should like to thank Susannah Frearson and Heather Evans for their proactivity and professional guidance throughout, and the editorial and production teams at Routledge who have supported us in bringing our book to life.

We also want to acknowledge and thank all our clients for, without them, there would be no stories. You have all been at the centre of our professional lives and we have grown together – it has been an honour and a privilege to work with you all.

We wish to thank Mark Hesslewood for his relentless commitment and generosity of spirit, which has enabled us to complete this manuscript.

In addition, there are several people who are not directly connected to this work to whom we are deeply grateful – namely, the many teachers, trainers, coaches and supervisors from whom we have learned. You have all helped us shape and make sense of our stories. If, as the old saying goes, judge yourself by the company you keep, we must be blooming amazing and we are appropriately humbled!

Heartfelt thanks go to our families and friends for your love, belief, generosity and patience – you know who you are.

Confidentiality

The stories in this book have been inspired by coaching work across the entirety of our coaching careers. That said, we have taken great care to ensure that the anonymity of our clients and the specifics of the coaching conversations are protected.

Foreword

This amazing book follows the journey of two highly experienced coaches, told from their fragilities, challenges, joy and despair, offering insight, signposting the road from novice to master coach. I certainly wish this type of material had been available to me when I became a director and choreographer when I was 30 years old, when my career as dancer was coming to a natural end and I was searching for another career in the business. I knew it had to involve leadership of some description and coaching, but where does one start?

Many of the books on coaching are focused on 'how to . . .' or on academic research that leads to conclusions and 'positions'. There are very few books that talk from the experience of a coach. This book salutes the development journey of a coach and tells real-life stories from the coach's mind-set which resonate and reflect the novice-to-master journey. Its purpose is to give insight and encouragement to developing coaches, stimulating competence and raising the professional bar. I recognise the need for dedication and practice with commitment to learn, improve and excel.

Karen Dean and Sam Humphrey have done a FAB-U-LOUS job in bringing the reader closer to an understanding of what 'really' goes on in the minds of coaches and helps the reader share the values of personal experiences from real people in their prospective fields. It's a great book for anyone wanting to develop both coaching and personal leadership skills so you can truly be that confident and inspiring person you know you are.

Craig Revel Horwood
Director, Choreographer and *Strictly Come Dancing* Judge

Preface

'I can't be the only one feeling like this!'

Our intention is to offer our coaching stories. We trust that some of these may resonate. We imagine that you might make connections with them and forge your own meaning.

Coaching can be an isolating and lonely profession, especially when work eludes us or when we have doubts about the way we have behaved. It takes humility and courage to be with ourselves compassionately. If we accept that there is purpose in these experiences, the stepping stones to our greater potential might be revealed.

In all the years we have been coaching there have been highs and lows or, as we choose to call them, times of 'flowing' and of 'falling'. We share these with equal intent and transparency. They were all purposeful and, in so being, presented different opportunities for reflection and insight.

At times we felt shame and despair, embarrassment and naivety. In experiencing these feelings, we needed to bring humility and care for ourselves and respect for our clients. It was sometimes shocking. The force of our judgement and self-loathing was difficult to be with, but it was always worthwhile. We needed to be patient, allowing the evolution of our understanding. We found ourselves waiting with agitation and then stillness for the wisdom beyond.

There was great joy and satisfaction at each stage of flowing. We are mindful of the ego and the danger of its inflation. Therefore, in sharing our stories of flowing, we celebrate. We seek to deepen our learning, recognising the gifts and remembering our part in co-creating with our clients.

Our clients are central to our stories. We honour each one. We trust that we have been mindful of their needs in sharing our journeys. The stories are about how we experienced the coaching conversations and are not a commentary on our clients. We are not sharing confidential details unless we have sought explicit permission first. Clients are not identifiable. Occasionally a story will be a composite of several stories to protect our clients. Mostly they are crucible moments that led to the gold nuggets of learning.

When we first set out on our lives in coaching, we were younger, energetically enthusiastic and evangelical at times. This was a period of risk and reward. The art of self-reflection was a much-needed practice back then. The further we travelled with our clients the more discipline we needed. The more complex our work the more important it was to seek out a wise colleague or supervisor to support, manage and guide us. We are committed to exploring our work in this way. We still have a long distance to travel. Our work is compelling and self-defining and it sustains in many ways.

I thank Sam for travelling with me. Together we have brought a great variety of stories. Our styles are so very different and yet we are aligned with the values and ethics of our profession and we have respect for each other's perspective and approach. Writing this book has been a deeply rewarding adventure for which I am grateful.

Karen

'Of course, I am unique – just like everyone else!'

When I first started on this coaching path, I did not really know that it was coaching or that it had a name. It was something I did, a state I became and it seemed to work. When I got serious about it and got some training and structure and process, I realised how much of a novice I was.

The journey from novice to master is a unique experience for everyone. You learn techniques, process, structure, how to use different resources, and many, many other things about your chosen field. You discover more about who you are, what your purpose is, what you value, what you despise, what stirs you, what bores you and a great many other things about yourself.

Whether you are a dancer, an accountant, an athlete or a business coach, your journey will always start at being a novice and through hard work, training and experience you can reach the heady heights of master.

In my journey, I was fortunate to meet and work with many of the people who would be considered the pioneers of coaching: the practitioners who carved out the coaching niche, who established the sector and pushed it towards becoming a profession; the academics who embarked on establishing an evidence base for the work; and the professional bodies that wanted to create a profession with ethics, standards and integrity.

All of this contributed greatly to the resources available for coaches to develop. Training with standards and competencies, research to support techniques and approaches, all of this was great for my development as a coach. What was conspicuous by its absence was an opportunity to benchmark my journey from a 'being' point of view. I knew what skills and competencies I was meant to be demonstrating, but what of my being? How was that meant to develop? How did I know I wasn't neglecting that part of my development?

Karen's framework, the backbone of this book, gives us the opportunity to look at our development as a coach from a different perspective. Our stories illuminate each stage – warts and all – and we hope to give you a new lens through which you can view your journey. What would you have done in our situations? What stories would you tell at different stages? What highs and lows have been the most impactful for you?

You should also note that we have given a high and low example for each stage but this in no way represents the balance in our journeys – the highs far outweigh the lows.

We can see that the old guard are less figurative in the coaching world and a new wave is coming to the fore, who will undoubtedly challenge what has gone before and make changes to the shape and feel of the coaching world. We hope our book forms part of those changes.

Sam

Introduction

'Exceptional Achievement' model originated by Karen Dean

I have been working in the field of coaching for 27 years across more than 20 sectors, globally. This has brought me a wealth of experience of clients and other coaches in my supervision practice and from learning with my peers. I am always curious and find myself noticing patterns and themes that I test and interrogate.

In the evolution of my career before coaching, I attained Fellowship of the Institute of Medical Laboratory Sciences specialising in haematology and serology (pathology of the blood and the science of blood transfusion). The scientific rigour demanded in the investigation of such conditions has served me well. I studied at Nottingham City Hospital and at St Thomas' Hospital in London. It is significant that the scientific mind-set, structural approaches and relentless pursuit of understanding how something might work underpin my learning style and subsequent relationship with the world.

I then joined a well-known high street retailer in the discipline of commercial management in stores and then in head office, working in sales management and corporate marketing. This work demanded attention to detail and an urgency of approach, with people at the core of the business. Creative thinking and a capacity to develop appropriate solutions was a feature of this time. Moving toward supporting others to reach their own answers became a natural yet focused progression.

During this evolving work, and in my coaching, I have listened to and observed many thousands of people. I noticed how patterns and language repeated and how cycles of emotion and frustration appeared. Immersion in one client organisation, which commissioned 3,500 hours of coaching from me, became my 'laboratory' for distilling my own theoretical framework. I tested this complex model with over 650 clients. A treasured few wrestled with my hypotheses in precise detail and supported me in validating my thinking. I owe them my gratitude and eternal respect.

I named the model that crystallised the 'Exceptional Achievement' model'. This model had 66 elements connected in a whole system of links and loops of language and states of mind. This complexity was then expressed in three layers as 'latent potential, exceptional achievement and realising potential'. This model is not the right answer to anything; it is a lens through which I have looked and offers a way of talking about the human condition.

In this book, we have used the framework to identify 12 stages on the journey from novice to master coach. These give rise to progressive touchstone moments throughout Chapters 1–12. In working with Sam, we could set out the intention of each chapter. We believe the learning pathway is apparent in how the bar is continually raised, highlighted by the increasing depth and sophistication shared in these stories: the highs and the lows. We have included short reflections after each story, in the form of 'What I wish they had told me' and 'What I wish I had asked'. These musings delivered learning and purpose for us both as we noticed key threads or themes, which certainly had meaning for us, and that we are willing to share.

Finally, we have offered established theories and models that speak to the themes arising. They close this book and yet they may open new avenues for you to explore further. It is your choice. We trust we have stimulated your thinking and stirred your emotions as you consider your own impact.

Part I

Setting out

Setting out

Chapter 1

Commitment

A decision to set out on a coaching journey, connecting, learning and growing

Flowing

I had decided to learn a new skill. I cannot say that I was particularly diligent in sourcing the trainer or the content. It was rather a spur of the moment thing on the recommendation of a well-respected friend. A course spread over six months, taking in several long weekends. Practising in between. A programme shared with 120 other delegates. I remember thinking, 'Oh crikey! That's a lot of people' and concluding that 'the trainers must know what they're doing'.

I rose early, sneaking about in the dark, walking on tiptoe not wishing to disturb my two young boys. I was curious, anxious, excited and cold. The outfit was a bit of a challenge. What should I choose so that I was putting my best foot forward and most likely to win friends and influence people? I believe it was jeans, shirt, blazer and ankle boots. My make-up was applied as diligently as always. After all, my Mum always remonstrated: 'You're not going out without your lipstick on, you're far too pale.'

I came from a mining village on the Nottinghamshire/Derbyshire border. My parents aspired to home ownership by working hard and being determined to achieve their dream. Indeed, my Mum went back to work when I was two years old, which was unheard of in her family of ten siblings, eight of whom were girls. Hard work paid off and my parents bought their brand-new house when I was eight years old. I had to leave the village school while the house was being built. I was bereft every morning, after a long and tedious car journey, to be walking through the gates of my fine new junior school.

The days began with much sobbing in the miserable toilets. I knew no one. My class teacher, for some reason, despised me from the word go. It was a lonely first year, filled with the all-pervasive smell of hops from the adjacent brewery. In my world this fragrance is forever associated with the hollow ache of being excluded. The shame of not knowing how to spell 'razor' burns in me still. The despair and apparent ignorance of getting low marks for mental arithmetic tests has left its mark. I was the only one who didn't have a 'slipper bag' for my plimsolls and gymslip. I knew what it was to start from scratch, a year behind the rest of the class; they all knew their place and had a sense of belonging. At least I thought they did.

I cannot remember pondering on this early history as I travelled down to London on the train. I was sure that the course would be good and I would learn a lot. I was determined to make the most of it.

I smiled and grinned and nodded and enquired, mirroring with polite manners whoever crossed my path. I hated the vacuum flask that refused to pour and was determined to embarrass me. One hundred and twenty is an awful lot of people. The music swelled and blared out from the tinny speakers, 'thiiiings can only get **better**!!!!' What a call to adventure!

In the coming days I was enthralled by the host and tutor, I sat mesmerised by his sorcery. He was irreverent and candid. He expertly demonstrated the processes and skills we aspired to learn, displaying mastery, subtlety and humour. He mocked our 'performance anxiety' and pandered to our need for a big thick manual. He encouraged us to go beyond where we dared imagine in developing a deeper relationship with ourselves. He was courageous and kind, unafraid to call out the pattern or resistance.

His compassion unlocked and transformed the lives of many of us. There were tears, hugs, fear and great joy.

Yes, there was practice, practice, practice. I was naive. My sheltered girls' grammar school education had stood me in good stead until now. The other delegates were from all walks of life, all backgrounds, ages, nationalities, experience, religions, cultures and sexualities. It was stimulating, surprising and frightening. We were sharing our private and intimate stories in triads of learning. Exposing our vulnerabilities. Occasionally annoying the hell out of each other, with prejudices prominent, yet we ploughed on. It was the most thrilling and appalling experience. I shall treasure it forever. We said goodbye with love and humility, noticing everyone. A community had been created and it had thrived and flourished. I was part of that.

What I wished they had told me:

> That people could be surprising and have such strange ideas and assumptions

What I wish I had asked:

> How am I ever going to coach someone who is so very different from me?

Falling

I was an experienced coach. I must have been, I had been working as one for twelve years and seemed to be highly respected. I certainly had plenty of coaching assignments. Curious about how I might take in some professional development I looked for an interesting workshop. Spurred on by a recommendation from a couple of friends and fellow coaches I applied for a place on a one-day activity held in Hampton Court Palace. All was looking good; there were about thirty delegates, some of whom I already knew well or at least by sight. I was feeling confident and relaxed, anticipating the day's learning. Hugging and chatting, nodding and smiling, we settled into a circle and the day began.

The course was exploring how transactional analysis theory[1] (TA) and specifically the TA drivers[2] might result in the behaviours of the coach and client becoming problematic. This was a new area of study for me and I was listening carefully to understand the theory and to apply its principles in my work, particularly to increase my self-awareness. A lack of rapport in the client relationship can be a deal breaker; it doesn't lead to trust and can result in the client disappearing from the partnership.

It was time to have a go and practise with the framework. We were set up in a triad, three of us taking it in turns to be coach, to be client and to observe. I had noticed an attractive, alert-looking woman, who was articulate in the group. I'd decided she was my first choice to work with. A close friend of mine offered to join us. We shuffled our chairs, delaying the moment to begin.

I understand now that it is important to bring 'real stuff' to a coaching intervention, even if it is a learning or practice situation. Back then I was ignorant. The exercise had been set up for the client to choose a driver behaviour and to role play the consequences of this behaviour during the coaching. The coach was to deploy their best efforts to move the client forward.

Of course, it is no surprise to me now, as an experienced coach supervisor, that one's client can bring what is your worst nightmare, or certainly the very issue that currently plagues you in real life. Blissfully unaware and yet earnest in my desire to be a 'good coach', I opened with 'and what are you bringing to the coaching conversation today?'.

My articulate client began her role play: 'Well, I've got this friend and she's really depressed and she keeps ringing me and I don't want to be mean but it's dragging me down. It doesn't matter what I say to her, she keeps going over old ground. It's all because of her not being able to make up her mind about the relationship with her boyfriend. She just keeps going around in circles. I'm trying to be a good friend but she is overwhelming me and I'm getting worn out with it all.'

I acknowledged how difficult this must be for her and invited her to set out her goal. 'Well I don't know, but what I do know is I can't take it anymore. I'm so drained, it's exhausting. When I try to suggest something, she gets very irritable and I'm feeling so frustrated.'

'What have you tried?', I asked.

'I've tried everything and nothing works. I'm ready to give up with her and yet she is my friend and . . . .'

The conversation ploughed on relentlessly and no matter how I tried to reframe or elicit a future outcome the client was having none of it. That's the trouble with role plays; the client doesn't get a live response in their body or mind to the interventions offered. That was no excuse, however.

I had failed as a coach. Overwhelmed with doubt, I knew it had not gone well. There was the faintest vibration in the centre of my body. I had tried my best but the articulate woman had not budged. I was concerned that my friend had witnessed the session and that I certainly wasn't as good as my ego had led me to believe. The vibration then pulsed and my heart started pounding, my face was flushed and I was doubting my skill, and even my right to be there. The feedback was lost on me, I was panicking. I didn't want to be judged but I heard the verdict.

As we returned to the larger circle we were invited to offer our experiences of the exercise. Third to speak was my articulate woman. 'SHE made me feel dreadful, I was getting so depressed talking to her. I was only role playing but by the time we'd finished I felt awful. She made me feel worse and it didn't work for me at all.' She may as well have taken out a knife and stabbed me in the chest, piercing my heart and draining the life from me.

What I wish they had told me:

> That sometimes people have a need to diminish others even when they profess to be inclusive and generous.

What I wish I had asked:

> What are the rules around here?

Flowing

For as long as I can remember, I have held a self-perception that I am a bit academically stupid. I don't think I am stupid in other things, in fact I think I am rather quick in most other things. I learn words to songs and keep fit routines quickly, I have a great memory for trivia and can remember things that others find incredible – one of my party tricks at college was to recall what outfits the class were wearing the week before. I can turn my hand to most tasks and learn how to do them quickly and improve them too. This latter point was particularly helpful when it came to relating to the people I worked with in factories – as a manager, your credibility was huge if you could do what they did on the production line and do it better.

It took me years to recognise that I am not a conventional learner. I cannot take information in when it is read to me; I go completely deaf. I also don't take in facts or data that have no connection, meaning or immediate utility. School work was painful and revision even more so.

My way of learning meant that my school qualifications were poor and I was left with a nagging feeling that I was capable of more but, as I hadn't delivered it, I must be academically stupid. This then informed my approach to learning and I only really committed to practical-based training and learning, which involved role plays, activities and rehearsals, because I was good at that stuff.

I am married to a wonderful man who went to one of the best private 'boys' schools' in the UK (and possibly the world), spent time at Sandhurst and was an Oxford scholar – not bad for a stupid girl from a wee town in Scotland. He was, and still is, incredulous at my intellectual self-perception and often challenges, with irrefutable data, to demonstrate how warped and wrong my view is.

This finally played out when I was asked to enrol in a Professional Masters in Coaching. I had landed a wonderful role at a global consumer goods company as the Global Head of Coaching and knew that, as this profession was in its early stages of development, I ought to try to learn more about it. What I was not sure about was how best to learn about it. At the time, there were not as many coaching courses available as there are now and they did not have the rigour of professional body accreditation. Neurolinguistic programming (NLP)[3] was everywhere but I knew that learning a technique or approach was not what I needed to do this job well. Having gone on a taster session, I met a well-respected coach who contributed significantly to the coaching community. He suggested I join the second Professional Master cohort. He saw my spark and potential and encouraged me to consider doing the course. It was perfect for me.

A balance of practice and theory with some research thrown in – it would challenge me, stretch me and have immediate application to my role.

I went into such a flap. I am stupid, I could not possibly complete a Master's degree, especially not while working and being a mother to two small children. My husband was able to quickly cut through all my 'chicken doors' as he was almost at the end of studying for his MBA – while working and being the father of two small children.

I knew this was a crucible moment and that, if I was ever to live in harmony with my 'stupid' gremlin, this was an opportunity to make that happen, but I would have to fully commit – body, mind and soul.

So, I did. I embraced my stupid gremlin and invited him to join me on this journey, help me ask 'stupid' questions, sit with uncertainty and not knowing, and rejoice in our stupidity so we could learn.

I would love to say that I graduated top of my class or won a prize for advancing coaching beyond all possible thought, but that was not the case. I passed and I now know that it's OK not to know 'O' level maths or be able to relay all the important historical battle dates because I have a badge that says: 'this woman is clever'.

What I wish they had told me:

> Stupid need not be a steady state; you learn differently from others so how can you make that work for you?

What I wish I had asked:

> What other ways can we try to access my capacity to learn?

Falling

If I chose to learn something, I believe very strongly I should commit to it. I am the best person to have in the room if you are teaching because I will look at you, smile, nod and listen to what you are saying – every word of it. If I have committed to be there you will get my full attention and my full commitment.

In the early stages of my coaching journey, I took on some work coaching some middle managers in a small organisation. As it was a small organisation, the fees were much below what I had wanted to accept but I needed the work and so took on the assignment.

I can see that my commitment had shifted with this work. I had an increased focus on meeting my needs and a strong sense of this throughout the work. I can see that I did not treat this client with the same attention, respect or level of service as I did my other clients, and this was primarily because I did not feel I was being valued for what I was doing. As a result, I subconsciously did not send her notes of any kind after the sessions, I was inadvertently less prepared than I would normally be and I found myself clock watching to make sure I didn't overrun on my time.

Unsurprisingly, this client did not flourish in our sessions, we did not do brilliant work and our end-results were underwhelming. When she asked to move a session, I thought this an inconvenience – another indicator of not being valued. I noticed that I felt she was getting me 'cheap' and this should have resulted in her being more respectful of my time. Although my thoughts may not have been as clear as this, my sense of it was.

As a commitment junkie, I had at least committed to good supervision and was able to explore this lack-lustre assignment in depth.

I can still feel the deep flush of shame I felt realising that I had treated this client poorly, I had not committed to her success and needs; I had committed only to my success and, in doing so, scuppered any chance of achieving it.

What I wish they had told me:

> Don't take on work unless you believe your full worth is being recognised appropriately.

What I wish I had asked:

> How else can I feel valued in my work?

Notes

1 Transactional analysis is a theory about the way people develop and relate to themselves and others. It is a psychological approach that is used therapeutically and in a wide range of other fields. it was originated by the psychiatrist Eric Berne in the 1950s. See Part 5 of this book for further background.

2 TA drivers come from the original work of Taibi Kahler (Kahler and Capers, 1974). Hay (2009 [1992], 1997; Hay and Williams, 1989) introduced the term 'working styles'. These characteristic styles comprise 'Be Perfect', 'Be Strong', 'Please People', 'Try Hard' and 'Hurry Up'. Refer to Part 5, Chapter 13.

3 NLP was developed in the 1970s by John Grinder and Richard Bandler, and deals with the structure of our subjective experience. This includes how the brain maps it, what language patterns are used to describe this, with particular attention on sequences or patterns of thoughts and behaviours that repeat. A range of methodologies is offered for seeking change in thoughts and actions.

References

Hay, J. (1997) 'Transformational Mentoring: Using Transactional Analysis to Make a Difference.' *Transactional Analysis Journal*, 27(3), 158–167.

Hay, J. (2009) *Transactional Analysis for Trainers*, 2nd edn. Broadoak End, Hertford: Sherwood Publishing (1st edn 1992).

Hay, J. and Williams, N. (1989) 'The Reluctant Time Manager.' *Opportunities*, May.

Kahler, T. and Capers, H. (1974) 'The Miniscript.' *Transactional Analysis Journal*, 4(1): 26–42.

Chapter 2

Confidence

In the early stages of competency, deploying the tools of coaching with impact for the client

Flowing

The coaching profession was rolling on, gaining momentum. Accreditation bodies were hot on the heels of professionalism. I was aware that in the USA, Europe and the UK there were credentialed coaching courses that had been developed by committed and determined training companies: organisations that had demonstrated the necessary content and approach to be aligned and endorsed by those international bodies. At the heart of this process was a code of ethics and a set of expected competencies, prescribed by the professional bodies. They recognised coaching performance against a framework of increasing levels of skill, which could be consistently demonstrated.

I found a place for me to go to, to gain the necessary professional development as a coach.

During the programme I felt de-constructed and rebuilt, polished and buffed. It was like waking from a long sleep to a bright light, the shock of shielding my eyeballs bathed me in adrenaline. I was indignant at the cheek of invasion, which was cruelly unannounced, the reality eventually dawning that the light was on, it hurt and there was no going back. I was changed. It was apparent to me in this process where I had been going wrong. I had therefore reflected and evolved my work. New skills and insights were plentiful. I had certainly grown.

As I left the training course I knew they had turned out a more impactful and mindful coach. I graduated full of anticipation and enthusiasm, renewed and vigorous. One element had come home to me forcefully; it was the need for a contract[1] to set up the coaching conversation. My sense of the contract was of a co-created verbal agreement between the client and the coach. This ensured that a clear and specific goal was the aim of the coaching conversation. The most surprising piece was the part of the contract that explored what working together on this goal might be like. Initially I had felt embarrassed and awkward pursuing this line of questioning. 'What's the goal?' was fine. 'What's my role?' was a very different matter.

We were sitting in a square room with a deep-pile, silvery blue carpet. A cold, circular, green glass table hovered between us. The halogen lights of the tall elegant lamp in the corner illuminated the otherwise dim space. She was my client, vivacious, eager and nervous. We had not previously experienced a coaching session together and I was acutely aware of setting up for success. I know I was nervous too, wanting this to work well, and for us to move forward with confidence and trust in each other. This was important and I wanted to be her coach.

After going around the block a few times, the client became increasingly clear on what she wanted by the end of the year, in working with me. She wanted to find her voice as an influential player in the many lives she touched. I'm paraphrasing the outcome for the purposes of confidentiality and respect for this client. I then went into a well-rehearsed description of the coaching model I was offering. I was clear that this coaching would be non-directive.

'I believe in you and your capacity to find your own best answers. I am offering a space for you to fully think about what is going on and what you would like to change. I know that you will be able to come up with your own ideas and to decide what will work best in achieving your goals.' I was glad to have said this so clearly. I followed up with: 'I am not going to offer you input or ideas on what you might do. I will, however, ask you questions to guide the process and to provoke insights and options. I shall enable you to decide what you want to act upon.'

I saw my client's eyes widen as I said: 'so what do you want from me, given that?' I was expecting her to say, 'challenge me' or 'help me understand why I haven't done it before' or 'I talk too much and you need to stop me if I'm rambling on'.

Instead she said: 'I want you to give me advice and to help me get there.' I could hear the eager invitation as she fixed me with bright blue eyes and a smile to melt my heart.

I smiled back with warmth and from some luminous place within me I gently replied, 'I am not going to do that'.

I held myself calm and clear. 'What I will do is listen carefully. I shall tell you what I am noticing. I shall be curious and trust the questions that come to me. I am committed to your goals.'

In that moment I held my breath and time stretched out and a coaching alliance was sealed.

What I wished they had told me:

> There is a deep and intimate bond between you and your client. Be mindful of its fragility and vigilant in preserving its integrity.

What I wished I had asked:

> How do I remember to speak my truth when I'm afraid?

Falling

I remember the sense of evangelism rising in me, wanting to coach everyone on everything, at any time. I was fresh from learning new and stimulating things. I had some powerful tools in my armoury and I had already witnessed their impact. I knew what a great difference I could make. I had worked hard and I'd taken the feedback and made good use of it. I was a coach after all.

I was ambitious and I had set out my stall to coach executives who were leading big businesses. There had been many assignments already but none as big or as full of potential as this one. The head of human resources (HR) had positioned me in to meet all the top team, with a view to coaching each one of them in whatever direction they chose. This was in 1995 when coaching was new and, to the few who had been initiated, it seemed like a great idea. The HR lead was enthusiastic in offering this development package and had set up the appointments to kick off the process. The business was traditional in its sector and yet entrepreneurial in its spirit. I was quick to assume that an initiative like this would be welcomed. I also believed that there was buy-in and purpose to doing this programme. The clarity of what sort of purpose eluded me, because I hadn't asked questions such as:

> 'What do you want to achieve for your business?'
> 'What makes this initiative important at this time?'
> 'What outcomes do you expect from coaching these leaders?'
> 'What impact do you want them to have?'
> 'What does success look like?'
> 'What does this mean for the culture of your business?'
> 'In what way have you involved any stakeholders?'
> 'How does coaching support your business strategy?'
> 'How might this programme impact your customers?'
> 'What if the Executive is not ready to engage with this investment?'
> 'What are the ethical boundaries here?'

These questions now roll off my tongue. Back then I had given no thought at all to the impact of my presence and my work. All I knew was that there were a lot of them and this was a brilliant opportunity to coach some bright guys. They were all guys. This would bring me some great fees.

I was a good coach and I had some powerful tools. What could possibly go wrong . . .?

He walked in, stepping lightly on his neat well-heeled shoes. His frame was big and his stomach parted the waves of air as he majestically crossed the room. I extended my hand to shake his. He left me hanging there before reaching out his small stubby-fingered palm to clasp me a little too tightly. I saw his eyes flicker over me and, in that moment, he was jury, judge and hangman. He wasn't going to make it a pleasant interlude and he was definitely going to make me, the confident coach, pay.

'What am I here for?' which exposed me to the first pitfall: Had he been briefed and how? 'Who are you?', which is rather a challenging question in the opening two minutes. 'Why would I want coaching?' Which is the question I wished I'd asked before he beat me to it.

'What qualifications do you have to work with me?' Well I had an answer to that but he wanted evidence and measures and impact and testimonials and nothing I said seemed to land. 'Had I brought any references?' Well of course I hadn't!

'I have been very successful and I have no idea what difference you can make to me.'

In effect he was determined to undermine my potential role in every way. I was at a loss. Without the clarity of outcome and his part in that, of course I could not fight my corner. On reflection having a fight with a potential client on first meeting seems like a recipe for disaster. I was then so concerned about failing to engage him that I failed to engage him, at all.

Many of the remaining initial conversations went very well and I tried to dismiss the impact of the encounter with that 'majestic emperor'. Sadly, he spoke loudly and relentlessly at the next executive board meeting. By the sheer force of his personality he insisted that my services were not required. There was unsurprisingly very little appetite to override his arguments. His ego prevailed and was preserved. Mine, on the other hand, took a serious beating. I did live to fight another day. I understood that I needed more than a few powerful coaching tools to be successful in the executive arena. Remember, this was a time before the coaching wave had swelled to significance and I had been adrift in a dinghy, which was soon holed and sinking, almost beyond repair. I needed to fire a distress flare and signal for a bigger vessel to come to my aid. Where was my coaching supervisor all those years ago, when I really needed her wisdom and support?

What I wished they had told me:

It is not just about you, so be prepared, strive for clarity and know your limits.

What I wish I had asked:

How do I understand as much as possible about this opportunity? What are the risks that I need to mitigate?

Flowing

In my learning, I have always found it important to see what good looks like. Having embarked on my Masters, I was loving the opportunity to transfer what I was learning on the programme directly to the work I was doing in a global consumer goods company. An imperative for me in this role was to 'fix' some problem encountered on our flagship leadership programme. A review had shown several things to resolve including some aspects of the coaching. The coaches' intent was not in question but their management of boundaries was and, had they had a better understanding of this and been in some form of supervision to ensure oversight on the work they were doing, then they may have been aware of the potential harm they could have caused and taken an alternative approach.

As a result of the review, it was agreed to 'properly' assess our existing coaching supplier list to ensure we could demonstrate a duty of care to both the executives the coaches would be working with and to the coaches themselves.

The assessment really was a belt and braces activity – a two-hour briefing on what the assessment was and why we were running it, a pre-assessment questionnaire, a full day of assessment and a 90-minute follow-up debrief.

In designing the assessment process, we agreed that what was most important was to see the coaches in action. Did they know what they were doing? Could they articulate what they were doing and why they were doing it that way? And finally, could they do it?

Having the opportunity to watch some of the world's best coaches through this process was, without doubt, one of the most profound learning experiences I have ever had. Watching a series of masters at work was joyous. The process enabled the coaches to articulate what their work was and then create space for them to demonstrate their ease with their craft. Although many were not natural presenters, most articulated their coaching approach and framework with wisdom and passion. To then watch this come to life in a 'real' coaching session was sublime; they had fully integrated who they were with what they practised and I watched it happening.

The experience of seeing less masterful coaches in this process was also a fabulous learning experience. I saw first-hand the impact of over-confidence, ego and, in some cases, a lack of humility in the coach and the coaching experience. Some blagged their way through their frame-work and some contradicted themselves, clearly not fully understanding the stage they were at in terms of their capability and boundaries. In most cases, it was the more inexperienced coaches who floundered in this pro-cess. I could relate to their euphoric enthusiasm for coaching and to their lack of coaching experience.

Seeing what good looked like then helped me manage my ego and euphoria. I could place myself in a coaching pecking order of compe-tence and experience. I knew that what I was doing was good and, more importantly, safe, and I had a picture of what I could aspire to. A won-derful check and balance on my confidence.

What I wish they had told me:

Often, good enough is good enough.

What I wish I had asked:

Where does a master go next in their coaching journey?

Falling

Stasis is my dread and has the biggest impact on my confidence. No change, no difference, no better off than when you started are all things I fear my clients will experience in working with me.

After having qualified in a new psychometric tool, I recall working with a client who wanted to improve how she led and managed her team. At this point, I can see that every client had a nail to work on because I was turning up with a hammer. I suggested we use this instru-ment to explore her type and think about how this might impact her leadership of the team. This client was not convinced about the instru-ment so was sceptical about it, but I suspect she felt unable to reject my puppy-like enthusiasm for it and agreed to go on with it. In the debrief, finding her best-fit type was impossible. She was not convinced she had a preference for one over the other and continued to relate context and purpose to how she would behave in different situations. It became blindingly apparent that she was getting no value from the session and was becoming increasingly irritated with me pushing on with this, as she saw it, ridiculous report.

I could feel my confidence draining out of me. I tried to convince her that the report had value but, in reality, it was me I was trying to convince. How could this wonderful tool, which I had spent a week learning, not be delivering the insight goodies I knew it could.

Having started the decline in confidence of the tool, I then turned my attention to my coaching and my inability to create value for my client. At this point of realisation, I blushed because I knew I was doing bad work and potentially damaging my relationship with this client.

In salvaging this one in supervision, I talked clearly about how this had so badly affected my confidence and I was worried about using the instrument again, worried about what my next session with this client would be like, how embarrassed I was, etc. etc. My supervisor looked at me and said: 'You do have great confidence. Listening to you describe how this played out for you, you clearly have confidence in your lack of confidence.'

Making me see this and feel a different type of confidence opened my eyes as to how I could work better with clients. Paying attention to what is being communicated rather than what is being said is vital if a coach is to have confidence in their work.

What I wish they had told me:

Celebrating is not boasting.

What I wish I had asked:

Is it OK with you if we stop?

Note

1 Contract: in coaching this is a mutually created verbal agreement taking account of the procedural, logistical, financial and ethical processes. Underlying all of these is the psychological contract, which is designed to mitigate disappointments and to manage expectations. This pays attention to the needs of both parties and is explicit about what will happen to ensure success in coaching, as well as what might get in the way and how this might be handled if it occurs.

Chapter 3

Ease

Consciously working with precision, yet lightly manoeuvring with the client's outcome in mind

Flowing

Ease for me is about the natural fluidity of the way in which I work with a client. Both of us honoured, respected and valued in the process. I pay attention to what I am hearing and the way in which I am hearing it described. We settle into a generative groove, which moves the conversation forward, coming ever closer to what the client wants.

A skill that I value highly and that resurfaced as I grew up was my capacity to hear every word another person said. This is both a joy and a curse and I found myself 'talked out' and exhausted in the early days of coaching. I was sometimes overwhelmed with detail and yet still able to remember most of it.

I say this capacity resurfaced because there was a time in my early career when it had gone to sleep. I was a retail manager where speed of delivery and appropriate attention to the commercial process and customers were expected. The environment was paternal and demanding. I was a quick thinker and had no idea how strongly my picture thinking drove my behaviour. I would finish someone else's sentences because I'd already got 'the picture' and did not have the patience to listen to their story, and ignored the opportunity to understand what was important to them. I behaved with arrogance, believing that I was right, and I had the determination to get my own way. I was very successful and certainly met the expectations of the firm. I'm not sure what some of my colleagues must have experienced. On reflection, I imagine they were subjected to quite a degree of control and felt ignored by me.

One day, on a personal development programme, I realised how poor my listening had become. This may have developed when I was very young, when the harsh tones of others in the throes of disappointment in me would have stung deeply. It may have been further reinforced in school.

Who knows? What mattered most was that I realised that I loved hearing what others said and that I had closed down a whole channel of high-value sound. I was shocked and saddened to understand this. I had a choice and I decided to build that listening muscle and reverently coax it to full strength. This took a long time. I began by actively concentrating fully on every word of a talk radio programme. I listened attentively to the news. I stopped rushing and pushing and let the sound come to me. Gradually my ears opened and I began to notice the subtlety and nuance of voice tone, volume and pitch, and eventually I developed an awareness of the way someone was breathing. All of this and the specific words that were used. Eventually I heard some words even more loudly and they struck me as significant and made me curious. They fed my questions and informed my awareness of someone else.

This played out in a first coaching session with a client who was particularly technical in a scientific field. We had talked through more details about our contract for working and had progressed to exploring where she wanted to get to by the time we had finished the programme of coaching. I asked permission to capture the things that mattered most to her. I described this intention or outcome as her 'desired state'.[1]

'What do you want to be seeing, hearing, feeling or thinking by the time the coaching investment is complete?' I then sat still, patient and believing in this intelligent, resourceful, fine woman in front of me. As she began to speak I captured exactly the words she uttered, instinctively, once her thoughts had settled into the best place. Delicately she populated the conversation with her future desires and I accepted them exactly as they were expressed. It was magical. Each element did not arrive fully formed and I remember asking 'in what way?'. Also 'What makes that important?' or 'What else?' I was as mindful of the quality of sound in the way I asked the questions as I was sensitive to her voice. Occasionally I heard her arguing with herself or, when in conflict, searching for the best and most accurate description. I could hold that space and with clarity increase her awareness of how she was expressing herself.

A most valuable lesson in learning through this conversation was when she gave me her first thoughts as 'I don't want . . .'. I noticed and respected that her technical mindset was always looking for the gap, the thing that didn't work, the problem that needed fixing. I explained to her 'your brain probably does not understand English grammar. It will connect to the very thing you are trying to avoid'. I demonstrated by saying 'try very hard not to think of a warm yellow sun'.

Firmly and gently I then asked her: 'If you don't want to be a poor presenter, what do you want instead?'

'I want to speak with authority and confidence', she replied smiling at this new thought. We were working together, and she was setting her direction with clarity and specificity.

What I wish they had told me:

Use all your senses wisely.

What I wish I had asked:

What do I say to my client when I'm overwhelmed with words?

Falling

I was sitting with a young man who was tall and willowy with hair that was ruffled and rebellious. He had not asked to be coached. He was part of a roll-out of a coaching opportunity that his company thought would be good for him. There had been very little briefing about what he might expect and it was my job to drive value in 90 minutes. I felt considerably older than him. I was smart and well groomed, in a good quality outfit.

He was using very few words and picking the quick of his nail beds. He seemed to be finding it difficult to sit comfortably and yet draped himself in the chair with his legs stretched out. I was upright, keen eyed and fixing him intensely with my professional look. The more uncomfortable he seemed, the more rigid and less approachable I became. I had fixed in my mind that it would be good if I guided him to an outcome for the coaching. Sadly the 'What do you want?' question was not well timed or best placed. How could he possibly know what he wanted when he didn't even understand what coaching was or how he fitted into this situation or whether it was even worth him bothering?

As I am writing this I am acutely aware of this young, creative, talented youth who found himself 'locked' in a room with a capable older woman, who may have been more like his mum than a fellow traveller on his life's journey. He wanted to bend the rules, to think of a better way, to be spontaneous, and I was clearly giving him no indication that I was a good partner in that. I clung to his sparse words and dissected them with 'Who's to blame?', 'What went wrong?', 'What could you have done differently?' There was no contract. I was clinging to a questioning process that I had heard in an NLP workshop, moving 'problem' to 'outcome'.[2] It was an effective pattern, which I had used before to good effect. This was my driftwood and I was hanging on for dear life as he sent waves of resentment my way. I lost my capacity to re-group, to be clear about what I was noticing, to let him choose the direction of the conversation. I felt clumsy and awkwardly old.

Strangely I know now that I am creative and flexible and can be spontaneous and freeing. This way of being had deserted me and I became more parental as the minutes ticked by. It would have been useful to notice how far from my usual style I had strayed. The coaching questions would surely save me!

I understand the importance of putting the client at the centre of the coaching, working on their agenda. With that man I was deconstructed and became fixated on sticking to my guns, regardless of the lack of trust or mutual recognition. Sticking to a pattern of questions when I don't even have permission to work with someone is pretty poor.

I did not have a coaching supervisor at that time. The memory of that session has stayed with me for many years. I suspect, having written this story, that I might raise it with my supervisor at our next appointment. That will be very useful and I shall grow as a result.

What I wished they had told me:

Assumptions and projection destroy rapport.

What I wished I had asked:

When I can't Be Perfect[3] should I Try Harder?[4]

Flowing

Many will recognise this in the competence learning model[5] as the third stage – conscious competence. This is the stage of development where you know what you are meant to be doing and you can do it without too much effort.

When I first learned about the GROW[6] model, I was a young human resources (HR) manager and saw it as a tool, a process and a structure to navigate a conversation about performance. I had no idea at that time that I would become a coach and would rediscover GROW in a different way.

The next time I met GROW, I had been accepted as a member of the internal coaching faculty at a global consumer goods company; we had our training in a number of different coaching models and GROW was one of them. I knew the model and what the letters stood for and that all you had to do was ask vaguely sensible questions at each stage. However, my eyes were opened to thinking about being a coach and not just doing coaching. GROW suddenly looked different, more challenging, more daunting and more important.

We did a lot of observed practices, which I found excruciating, but it meant that I grew into a being and doing coach. When I did my Masters, we didn't really play with models like GROW; we were exploring different models of coaching such as existential coaching, cognitive–behavioural coaching, gestalt coaching, etc. It was only when I joined the faculty of an organisation that trained coaches that I became re-acquainted with GROW. Early on in the Business Coach Programme, the tutor is required to demonstrate GROW with one of the participants. At first, I was horrified at the thought of doing this. I became self-conscious at the thought of it and imagined all forms of failure or disaster that would embarrass me and ruin the learning experience of the participants. I can recall doing my first fishbowl[7] and how terrified I was but I got through it and did a half-decent job of it. It was a bit clunky, but I did what I needed to and without dramatic incident, so I chalked that one up as a success.

I can't remember how many fishbowls I had done, but I do remember that there was a point when I was doing one at which I became aware, only for a moment, that I was at ease with it. In the debrief, my participants all commented on how easily I moved between the different stages, how effortless it looked. 'How did you know when to move on?' asked one of the participants. In thinking about this, I knew I didn't just 'know'; there were signs, tangible cues that told me, and I realised I was skilled enough to notice them and decipher them, which in turn enabled me to make an informed decision about what to do next. It was not some magic, ephemeral, all-knowing thing; it was primarily about doing what I had been trained to do and being present enough to pick up the signs. I am not advocating that coaching is only about skill but, at this point in time, I knew I had the skill. I really enjoyed this point in my journey. Being consciously competent is a wonderful feeling. I knew I was good at what I was doing and that my client was getting value from it. One thing I recall from that point was how full my coaching toolkit was then. I was a bit of a magpie and loved repurposing tools, techniques, frameworks and models to add value to a client's agenda: using the McKinsey 7-S framework (Peter and Waterman, 2006) to help a client frame their personal direction, and using De Bono's Six Thinking Hats (De Bono, 1985) to help a client learn a way of developing empathy. I would use any tool in any way, with skill to help my client get what they wanted from the session.

I can recall being hungry for tools and how important it was at this stage to have a breadth as well as some depth to my repertoire. Knowing I had a huge arsenal of coaching tools to call on, and that I could consciously tailor it for my client, left me feeling good at what I did. This was coaching with ease.

What I wish they had told me:

The pain is worth the gain.

What I wish I had asked:

How can you keep this feeling?

Falling

I used to hate chemistry[8] sessions. I overthink them or I don't pay them enough attention or I prepare too much or not enough for them. I wear the wrong outfits, I say the wrong thing, I focus on the wrong things.

I can recall having a chemistry meeting with a potential client. I was meeting a lawyer and had been briefed as to what the coaching was intended to achieve, but I needed to be aware that he did not really know what coaching was.

I knew that credentialing was important when working with professionals, so thought I had better do a bit of that so that he would warm up to the meeting and me in the process.

So, I went on transmit. The chemistry session became more of a tutorial, an instruction manual of how coaching worked. I took my checklist of things to cover in a first meeting with me and suggested we follow that format. He, of course, agreed to this and sat patiently as I transmitted my point of view on what coaching was and wasn't, how I managed confidentiality, the logistics of the coaching, measurement, blah, blah, blah. Even I was bored saying it, so goodness only knows how the poor chap felt listening to it.

At the end of it I asked if there was anything he wanted to know to which he replied, 'No'.

Technically, I was brilliant. I covered everything one 'should' cover in a chemistry meeting and I left him with no unanswered questions – but only if those were the things he wanted to know!

When I reflected on my experience, I could see that it was clunky, clumsy and clinical. I showed nothing of me and what I was about. The impression I would have left of what it was like to be coached by me would have been similar to what it would be like to be coached by a stereotypical army instructor barking orders and issuing directives.

Not quite the coaching style to which I was aspiring. Needless to say, I didn't get picked and, worse, got no feedback as to why.

After a heavy exploration of chemistry sessions with my supervisor, I realised that what I needed to do was focus on giving the client an experience of what it would be like to be coached by me. As a primarily non-directive coach, I started to attend chemistry sessions with a new freeing abandon – I would let the client direct the session.

This led to another series of unmitigated disasters.

This time, I was too unstructured in my approach; I gave my clients too much space to determine the agenda for our time together and this scared my potential clients. The feedback I got was that I seemed like a lovely person, they got on with me really well, but they didn't know what working with me would look like or what they would be doing.

Needless to say, apart from worrying about getting work, I realised that this either/or position was not helpful and that a both/and was required if I was to look and feel at all at ease.

What I wish they had told me:

You can't control chemistry.

What I wish I had asked:

What does exploring authentically look like?

Notes

1 'Desired state' is an adaptation of an NLP process to support a client to become clear about their outcomes and how they would recognise their achievement and mitigate any necessary obstacles, using positively framed language.
2 The NLP process of 'problem' to 'outcome' sets out two contrasting frames of thinking, from failure and blame to what might work better instead.
3 'Be Perfect' is one of the working styles described by Julie Hay (Hay and Williams, 1989; Hay, 1997, 2009 [1992]) from the original work of Taibi Kahler, in Kahler and Capers (1974).
4 Try Hard is another working style.
5 The Competence Learning Model was first articulated by Martin M. Broadwell (1969). It was later described as 'Four stages of learning any new skill'. This theory was developed at Gordon Training International by its employee Noel Burch in the 1970s.
6 GROW is a coaching model developed by the late Sir John Whitmore (1992) and colleagues. The GROW model is detailed in his book, *Coaching for Performance: GROWing People Performance and Purpose*. See Part 5 Themes and theories).

7 Fishbowl is an observed activity where a live activity, such as a coaching session, is performed in front of a group of observers.
8 Chemistry is the word used to describe the rapport between a coach and a client.

References

Broadwell, M. J. (1969) 'Teaching for Learning (XVI)'. *The Gospel Guardian* 20(41), 1–3a.

Hay, J. (1997) 'Transformational Mentoring: Using Transactional Analysis to Make a Difference.' *Transactional Analysis Journal* 27(3), 158–167.

Hay, J. (2009) *Transactional Analysis for Trainers*, 2nd edn. Broadoak End, Hertford: Sherwood Publishing (1st edn 1992).

Hay, J. and Williams, N. (1989) 'The Reluctant Time Manager.' *Opportunities*, May.

Kahler, T. and Capers, H. (1974) 'The Miniscript.' *Transactional Analysis Journal* 4 (1), 26–42.

Whitmore, J. Sir (1992) *Coaching for Performance: GROWing People Performance and Purpose*. London: Nicholas Brealey.

Part 2

Doing

Part 2

Doing

Chapter 4

Proactivity

Curiosity to explore mutual creativity, pushing the boundaries for fresh experiences

Flowing

There was a client I worked with who had a really juicy agenda to work on and wanted to be coached. She had a brain the size of a planet and could run rings around most people intellectually. I loved working with her because she was a sponge and I trusted her intellect enough to know that working on her agenda in a very different way was what she needed to do if she were to make a shift.

We used to meet at her offices in one of the posh meeting rooms. They were rather staid, traditional rooms with no charm or character in how they were decorated and with glass panels. This meant passers-by could see us in conversations and I could see that this made her uncomfortable. It was not great for me either because knowing I can be seen or heard with a client attacks the degree of safety I feel for my client, the work we can do and myself.

I suggested that we meet outside the office, perhaps in a meeting room nearby, so we could have better levels of privacy and a different vibe. We next met in a private meeting room near to her offices and the difference in her demeanour was palpable. She looked more relaxed, talked more freely and was more present in the session. I pointed this out to her and she could see the change herself. Her new-found confidence to be coached gave me permission to try some new things with her.

I used a number of different tools and techniques such as a set of picture cards to explore her objective in the session, Post-It notes to create a network map, and a collection of wooden dolls to work through a particularly tricky meeting she had coming up. We both loved all of this work as it turned up new insights for us both. She was up for almost any approach I brought to the session. She so valued the opportunity to look at something from a different point of view or perspective and in a way that she would never have thought of herself.

Central to her agenda was the ability to empathise in conversations with people and to do so authentically. She could not understand why people needed or valued this and, no matter how much forensic analysis she did, she could not figure it out. An 'aha' moment came when I asked her to try an empty chair activity. The notion of literally sitting in someone else's chair/shoes seemed very strange to her but she was willing to try it.

Within minutes of sitting in the first chair, the scales fell from her eyes. It was a real epiphany for her. She learned that empathy is not agreement or approval but understanding and acknowledgement – something she had not been able to define through her data-based analysis of a situation.

Her willingness to let me nudge her in a different direction meant that I could bring a different approach, energy and experience to our sessions.

My dolls are one of my most provocative tools. I have a series of 5-inch wooden dolls wearing a number of different outfits – a nurse, a doctor, a firefighter, a farmer, a school teacher, a thief, a pirate, a fairy –about 30 of them.

I don't use them with every client and I don't even mention them when people ask how I work and what techniques I use because I tend to think people need to be warmed up to the idea of them.

I worked with one client who seemed to be getting value from our time together. I shared with him that I had a broad repertoire of tools and he asked me to bring something 'really out there' to work with when we next met.

I thought of the dolls and knew, at that moment, it would be great. I knew, because I felt a flutter in my stomach, a rise of excitement at the prospect of using the dolls.

In the next session, I tipped them on to the table. I invited him to pick one that represented him in his current situation and one that represented his boss – his challenging relationship with his boss was the focus of the coaching work. I had barely finished talking when I was almost pushed out of the way so he could start playing with them. The dolls unblocked something in him and allowed him to view his situation in a completely different way. They helped him articulate his position, explore his boss and peers' situation, and come up with new ideas and thoughts about how he could be different and change his situation. The flutter in my stomach had been right, and my curiosity to help him explore his situation in a new way resulted in a very different outcome for him.

What I wish they had told me:

> When you have a sharp intake of breath moment, you are doing good work.

What I wish I had asked:

> Where do I go when I am not curious?

Falling

One client with whom I was working was really struggling with her topic – a very toxic working relationship. She was bright and had done all the rational analysis one could on the topic and, in doing so, found only more reasons for why she was right and her colleague was wrong. This binary context of the relationship was making things worse.

I explained to her that we could try looking at this in a totally different way and suggested an empty chair activity. I was so fuelled by the opportunity to experiment that I lost sight of my client and how she was feeling about the activity. It was rather ironic that I lost my empathy in trying to help her with hers.

As I described the role of each chair and how the activity would run, I turned to look at her and saw how terrified she seemed.

I asked her what was going on and she flew into a rage. She told me she had never heard of anything so ridiculous and how could this possibly help her in her current situation – I had allowed my excitement to experiment to take precedence over her needs and feelings in the moment.

As I was committed to my suggestion, I encouraged her to give it a go and see what happened, feel what came up. Needless to say, my push was met with an equal resistance – the immovable object had met the unstoppable force.

We both felt embarrassed, helpless and angry – which is of course all data but, in the moment, it was awful.

My lack of experience in handling this situation meant I rushed it, stole responsibility for it and ultimately did it badly. Our relationship never really recovered after that and our coaching work was quite transactional.

What I wish they had told me:

> If it doesn't go to plan, be sincerely sorry.

What I wish I had asked:

How do I really know if I have permission?

Flowing

My client was practically creative. She was incredibly driven by her feelings and indeed her felt sense of the world. Too many words were overwhelming for her. She found the description of what was important for her difficult to isolate. I observed that the language she was choosing was helping her toward her goals and yet I had an impression that there was also frustration. I offered this observation to her:

'I am noticing that when you are thinking and you then speak there is pent-up energy there. I'm experiencing this as frustration. Is that useful to know?'

I sat patiently while she responded to this insight, mindful that I could be completely off the page, and yet glad that I had found a way of sharing what I was noticing.

'I do find it frustrating. I can't find the words to say what I want to say. I have such a lot of feelings about everything and words won't do. It's always been difficult for me to say what I'm feeling. I know you've said that the conversation is all about me and my ideas. The trouble is that I've got loads of ideas and I just can't find the right words. This really matters', she said tight-lipped.

'I'm hearing that you have loads of ideas and not saying them is frustrating', I echoed. 'What do you do with your ideas when they do come?' I asked.

'Oh, I draw them, or sew them, or make them or just play with stuff I have hanging around.' She was more animated, upright and leaning towards me. Her hands were working together as if she was building something right in front of me.

'You look like you are building something right there,' and I pointed to a space where her hands had been active.

'Yes, yes it feels like I am, but I've no idea what!' and she dropped her hands into her lap again and frowned back at me.

'It seems that whatever it is might be useful now?'

'Well yes, I suppose it would,' she replied hesitantly.

'You said that you just play with stuff you have hanging around. In this cupboard I have some clay hanging around. It's not messy like pottery clay, it is more like plasticine. It is an offer. What do you feel about using that while we talk?'

She jumped up, 'in this cupboard did you say?', reaching for the door eagerly.

'Yes, that's the one. Get it out, it's right there,' I pointed to a bar of grey corrugated clay. 'You'll have to work it for a while as it's cold. The clay needs to warm up a little so it moulds better.' I followed her enthusiasm as she tore open the packet. I watched her knead the clay with swift, deft fingers, rhythmically rolling and pummelling. I could see the clay responding to her touch, the table becoming dusty. There was no stopping her and she began to create.

At first there was a cube and a flat plate-like shape. 'What do these represent?'

'I feel like I'm shut in a box. I often feel squashed because I can't say what I want.' She thumped the cube flat and matched the plate shape on the table. 'It feels like there's nothing to offer sometimes,' she added.

Then she bundled the clay together again and continued working, tearing off a fraction of the whole. She concentrated then upon figuring a small person, with hair and clothes and eyes. I continued to watch her, saying nothing. She was intent.

As she finished this I asked her: 'What do you notice about what you've made here?'

'She is really little. She looks nice. Oh! She hasn't got any mouth and no ears either.'

'What does that let you know?'

'That I don't think I've got them!'

'What impact does that have?'

'I stop myself saying stuff that matters.' She touched her chest as her eyes filled with tears.

I stayed quiet and still, saying nothing. I continued to watch her as she experienced what was important to her.

After a while she took up the clay once more and absent-mindedly pressed and pulled and moulded. She then began to pay more attention as she worked the ball of clay. After several minutes she placed the piece in front of her.

'I've no idea what that is.'

'What does it remind you of?' I prompted.

'Well it looks like a nut.'

'What sort of nut?' I asked gently.

'A walnut.'

'What does a walnut remind you of?' I asked once again.

'Oh my God! My brain! Oh God!'

'What's important here?' I said.

'I want one of those!'

'What if you had one?'

'If it looked like that then I'd be able to use all of it and not feel so stupid.'

'How would you feel instead?'

'It would be great,' and she went on to explain just how great it would be.

I particularly asked her to consider whether she wanted to see someone else who might help her understand where this came from and what else she might do about it. I was mindful of the fine line between coaching and counselling. What I did more than anything was trust my client's process. I witnessed her creativity and her capacity to discover the mindset that had stopped her fully being herself. Something had shifted and it was an honour to be with her.

What I wish they had told me:

> How incredible our brains are, how metaphorically and literally they behave, bringing simplicity to our ways forward.

What I wish I had asked:

> What does this work say about my capacity to be creative?

Falling

I was fresh from the NLP practitioner training. The tools had worked so well in the training room, my particular favourite was the 'circle of excellence'.[1] This was a guided process, where the NLP coach offered a way for the client to access their very best state, in order to achieve an important outcome that previously would have been challenging.

Of course, this methodology was relevant for so many of the clients I then met, that it became ridiculous. It popped into my mind so regularly that it was almost distracting. At that time, I was completely relaxed about suggesting a methodology, almost as if I were the expert on their experience and that I knew best what would be good for them. I had noticed that, provided I was in rapport with the client, then they seemed fairly compliant and willing to follow my lead. This is dangerous territory. Arrogance and a sense of powerful control lurked in the shadows, on the fringes of the conversations, tempting, brooding, pensive, ready to pounce.

There was a tall, athletic man who was experienced in his role and yet was hesitant to address a larger group of people, particularly if it was using the microphone of a public-address system. He looked as if very little would faze him and yet his fear of public speaking in this way was a real challenge. He shared his concerns and the 'circle of excellence' catapulted into my mind once again. Of course, I knew this was the right tool and this would fix the problem he was describing. It was unusual and different and was pushing the boundaries, and I knew it worked. So enthusiastic was I to take it out of my kit bag that I had stopped listening to my client.

'I think you should use the "circle of excellence" and this will set you up to do what you want in the best way you know how.'

The insistence on this tool as the right next step was, as I look back now, way too fast for comfort. I was not respectful of what my client might create to support himself. I did not even ask if it would be OK for him to have a go at this process.

'Please stand up and I want you to imagine you are drawing a circle out in front of you; this is your "circle of excellence",' I directed.

He stood up, hands lost by his sides, shoulders drooping. He looked pale now as I reflect and he seemed distinctly uncomfortable. However, I was well into my stride and ploughed on with the steps of the exercise. He was hardly enthusiastic about accessing a time when he had been calm, confident or clear. His eyes were flashing and darting although somehow his capacity to step into his resources had abandoned him. I found myself feeling frustrated and irritated, because I knew it would work if only he would just do it properly! Quite frankly by the time the exercise was drawing to a close he looked as if he was going to weep, from embarrassment or shame or shock, or perhaps he was feeling a combination of all three. This was certainly not my finest coaching session and I now feel those same three emotions as I share this.

I know now that my capacity to listen to and follow the lead of my client is paramount. He was the expert and I had a delicate role to perform in walking with him on his way to addressing his challenge.

The coach supervisor in me notices that I was probably playing a role that echoed the time, when he was a boy, when this had unravelled for him. I may have been reminding him of a goading teacher or a strict and impatient tutor, reinforcing the very thing that had caused him the issue in the first place.

Back then I was seduced by the power of the tool and its experimental nature. Quite frankly I wanted the kudos I perceived would be mine, once I had made my client better or solved his problem. A lesson in humility was overdue.

What I wish they had told me:

This is not just about following the steps in the manual; you need to tread with care.

What I wish I had asked:

How did you learn to be so sure of yourself?

Note

1 The NLP 'circle of excellence' is a process for finding and connecting the required inner resources to enable a person to move from their 'present' to their 'desired state'.

Chapter 5

Talent

Noticing evolution beyond technique, celebrating the unique approach

Flowing

My client was a dream client. He was in a very senior role, in an organisation with world-impacting purpose, he was open to coaching and determined to get value from it. In my book, I'm not sure it gets better than that.

We had great chemistry – lots of overlap, lots of difference – and I intuitively knew this would be a great assignment.

When we completed our work, we were reviewing what we had done and how we had worked together. My client turned to me and said: 'The best thing about working with you is that you make me feel comfortably uncomfortable.' At the time, I thought it was a 'nice' thing to say but, reflecting on it, I could see this phrase truly summed up my core coaching competence.

I can see that many of the adjectives I heard as a child related to this core competence. Grown-ups would use words such as challenging, insubordinate, cheeky, aggressive, impudent, provocative and difficult. Although I can see how the impact of my behaviour might result in being described in those words, my intent was mostly driven by an insane curiosity about things and a driven need for fairness.

As a child, my vehicle to deliver this intention came mostly in the form of unfiltered comment on a situation. My 'in the moment feedback' was a mix of observed data, my sense making of the data, and was, annoyingly for the receiver, often accurate. As this feedback had not been asked for, my lack of permission made my feedback seem predatory, so any good intention was invisible.

In starting work in the car industry, I found that some of the more stag-like, alpha male managers would sometimes seek me out and ask for feedback on what I had seen, in a particular meeting or conversation, about how they had contributed or behaved. I loved these types of conversations because I knew I had permission to say some things that could actually make a difference to this person and his relationships. The responsibility I had been given in those conversations was very different from other responsibilities. I knew I had been chosen for the conversation, given permission to share my observations and expected to say something that would be useful to them. These were not formally contracted coaching conversations but were close to the type of coaching work I love the most and know I can do well.

Having now got a taste for such conversations, I would try to create opportunities for these to happen. As I look back, I can see lots of damaged relationships littered behind me because I had not embodied the first part of my dream client's comment. I appeared to be on a mission to make people feel uncomfortable and forgot to pay attention to doing this in a way that was comfortable for them.

When I came to my first experience of coach training, I realised the need for and importance of safety. In my early days, I confused permission with safety and thought that, by asking clients if I could be really challenging and direct, that would make the coaching safe.

My next developmental moment on this topic came when I was working with three clients from the same organisation. The level of change the organisation was going through was huge and these clients were being beaten up by everyone on everything. In my contracting conversation with one, she talked about how she needed tough love to get her through the next few months. In that moment, I could see that, if I got the balance between the tough and the love wrong, I could damage her. This realisation was totally impactful on how I worked with her and changed how I coached forever. I brought a new compassion and a different form of diligence into my work that added hugely to my talent as a coach.

So, by the time I started working with my dream client, my core competence was better balanced and, therefore, more impactful.

I can still recall the detail of many of our sessions now – how in flow[1] we were both feeling palpable shifts in the room and knowing how my being and doing contributed to it.

Often, coaching results in your clients achieving things that they probably would have achieved anyway, but the coaching has helped them do it faster, better, to a higher quality, etc. This is very satisfying work and obviously adds value to the client and their organisation. That said, I think the really sweet spot in coaching is when your client can honestly say they have achieved things they would never have achieved had it not been for the coaching. I could see this happened for my dream client; I suspect it had a lot to do with how integrated I was in how I worked with him: a perfect paradox of comfortableness and uncomfortableness.

What I wish they had told me:

On its own, having permission to push doesn't make it safe to push.

What I wish I had asked:

How do I express my core competence with diligence and safety?

Falling

Then I thought I had another dream client. He was young, ambitious, considered high potential in his organisation and had a coaching agenda to work on.

I was excited at the possibility and feeling confident in my ability to do good work with him. At first, I experienced him as a little resistant. He was not convinced on the development points he had been given by his superiors, which were paradoxically playing out in this very conversation. I began to slow the conversation down to allow him to explore what was happening. The data was there in the room and, if he could see it and embrace it, we could get off to a flying start.

I tried numerous times to orientate him to see this data and, every time I tried, he only gave me more data to support the development points he needed to work on.

I thought I had a broad repertoire so I turned to some alternative frameworks and tools. He was willing to 'give them a go' and, every time I thought we were making some progress, he would slide quickly back to square one.

I spoke about him in supervision and left armed with more tools and techniques to try to prise him open. Every session would eventually fall back to the same place – square one.

I started to dread seeing him because I felt so useless. I wanted to blame him for it, but he had a coaching agenda and what looked like a willingness to be coached so, clearly, the fault was with me.

He could see I was getting exasperated at times and I often found I was having to give more attention to managing myself than I was to coaching my client.

I could not see where this was going to end up and feared that it was just going to get worse and worse. Not only did I start to worry about my sessions with him, but also got anxious about what he was saying to his coaching sponsor and how this would reflect on him and me.

I began thinking that I was not as good at this coaching lark as I thought I was and that, perhaps, I was punching above my weight. Working with this client felt like work, and hard work. I ground my way through the coaching assignment. By the end, I was in bits – not only did I feel my coaching had unravelled but everything around me had too. I was questioning everything – how I dressed, my business model, my 'right' to be doing this work. The negative impact of this work on whom I was as a coach was quite profound.

What I wish they had told me:

Sometimes you have to 'sack' your client.

What I wish I had asked:

How do I resource my client to resource me to help him?

Flowing

We were sitting in a minimal office space, few distractions, brightest daylight and stifling heat. The intensity of the meeting room mirrored the heightened concentration of my client. He was wrestling with matters of existence and purpose. He was seeking his truth and had invited me to walk that path with him. We had been working together for a while. He paid great attention to the process underlying our work, even while he had the capacity to reflect deeply in himself. It was a formidable talent. His capacity to think in many dimensions was both a joy and a stretch for me. This was a challenge I wanted to meet.

I was open to learning as much as possible at a crucial stage in my development, layering experiences, building confidence in my capacity and boosting my store of golden nugget moments for future reference. Such a nugget was revealing itself as we explored together.

I was watching his eyes, dark and quick. He was processing at great speed as each passing thought was completed and shared or filed for future reference. Occasionally he would step up and out of his chair and pace the floor, wrestling with the question I had posed or seeking the next valuable piece of his jigsaw. I was in such deep rapport that as he stood I would step up also, almost without noticing. I took my place beside him, occasionally asking permission to be on his left or his right. I did not insist on his eye contact, trusting that there was more than enough revealed by observing him at a distance.

I am not sure that my ability to set up the coaching contract was as well developed and sure-footed as I would have liked. At that time, I was more ignorant of how meaningful and essential a strong and explicit contract can be. It seemed good enough. We had a goal and we were used to our way of working.

I know, on reflection, that I was building a three-dimensional model in my head of the pieces he was offering and describing. I was gathering a sense of the whole and the connections that were revealing themselves. This enabled me to navigate the landscape of his responses intuitively and accurately. I was striving for, as Oscar Wilde said, 'the simplicity beyond complexity'. It did not seem to matter how much information he gave me, I was able to acknowledge what I had heard. He reflected on what I had played back to him, nodding as it landed in his awareness and then following the thread to the next insight. This informed my questions – revealed in me as instinctive waves of wonder.

Working as his coach I also needed to stay calm. Occasionally he would snap at me with withering words. I had a sense of this being another voice from within him – the critical, controlling, dismissive voice. The first time this happened I found myself holding my ground, keeping my voice firm, deep and direct. I was not going to be intimidated by this aberration in his style, that voice was useful and meaningful and held vital clues to his pattern. With clarity and courage, I asked him 'Whose voice are you speaking with?'.

This question threw him, interrupting his habitual responses to what the voice usually elicited in others. Rather than staying quiet and avoiding a confrontation or seeking harmony, I stood in my space and spoke with the authority that my role afforded me.

This was purposeful in me as his coach and delivered purpose for him in pursuit of his goal. 'My father, and I'm noticing that he was often dismissive. He was determined to stop me when I became too enthusiastic or was running away with too many crazy and irrelevant ideas.'

'What is the impact on you?'

'I am now feeling angry and sad, all mixed up,' he said.

This was a time when I became more fully aware that I embraced the system of what I was hearing, by building a model of how it made sense for me. I used this to guide my questions and keep me focused on my client's goal. I had the courage to stay in rapport, even when the client wanted to evoke a drama. This meant that the next insight could not be buried in distractions. It was acknowledged and the momentum toward the goal was maintained, with deeper insight and empowerment. The client understood that there were new and different choices to be made and he was free to choose.

What I wish they had told me:

> Coaching is a life-affirming, deeply validating interaction of great mystery.

What I wish I had asked:

How can I hold this joyful purpose at the centre of my life?

Falling

In my earlier coaching work the sponsor in an organisation would come to me with a request to coach a specific number of people. I would be coaching every person. The sponsor had built a relationship with me and trusted the connection. Very often a sponsor had very little understanding of coaching, yet he or she believed it worked. A coach should be able to work with anyone, was the received wisdom at that time, and that was OK then.

The coaching offers gradually became more sophisticated. Credentialing evolved in pursuit of quality professional practice and the mechanism of commission shifted. Increasingly, internal human resource (HR) professionals trained as coaches or had an interest in coaching. The more experienced of them, who wanted to embrace coaching and to have a more integrated coaching culture, took on the role of broker. The HR professional would interview prospective coaching clients to determine the client's goals, their style and preferences. They had taken on the task of allocating a particular coach from an external panel. This attended to the presenting or perceived need. Remedial coaching was more prevalent then and the client did not always come voluntarily; sometimes it was thought that they 'needed' a coach – which was a very different proposition.

The coaching profession moved on again and the concept of the chemistry session[2] became increasingly common. It certainly was in the coaching circles in which I moved. This was where a prospective client was given the opportunity to meet two or three potential coaches, which put the client in the driving seat. They could choose the coach with whom they connected the most. Each individual client had their own mechanism for making a choice. Sometimes the client would choose a coach with a similar style, someone who felt familiar. Alternatively, others would find someone they perceived to be very different from themselves – a coach whom they felt would present the most provocative challenge.

In the chemistry session, how could a coach discern the secret of the client's process? The client was the expert on their experience (I had certainly been told this repeatedly). It seemed that every coach had equally varied ways of conducting a chemistry meeting. I began to understand more about this phenomenon. In chatting with fellow coaches, either socially or as we shared our process in supervision groups, some of the mystery was revealed. There was typically a sense of the coach 'winning' or 'losing' the coaching assignment, with the predictable consequences from this frame of thinking. The coach rarely gave the client an experience of what it might be like to be coached by them. It seemed to be much more about whether the client 'liked' the coach, or whether they were 'good enough' which was an even more problematic mindset.

I had been evolving my own coaching philosophy and model. I was increasingly in touch with my capacity to clarify, simplify and be compassionately direct. I was offering my creative, intuitive, flexible interventions in flow with my clients. This felt precious to me and I was proud of my progress.

I was invited to meet a potential client. The sponsor had described him to me as a maverick in the organisation, very different from their cultural norm. He had been recruited to bring his difference. HR believed there would be value in offering him a coach who would partner with him to integrate well, while retaining his refreshing perspective.

The chemistry session was about to begin. I was sitting smartly in my suit, with the best matching blouse. I was breathing out slowly and for prolonged moments. This always relaxed my diaphragm and indeed my whole body. I took the time to fill my lungs with air that flooded my brain with oxygen. I wanted to be good enough, on top of my game.

Tucked in the top of my capacious handbag was a shawl, it had a pattern of medium-sized circles, regularly arranged in two tones of blue. My eyes are blue. This shawl was a gift from my mother who, a few months before, had died of breast cancer. This man could be a great client from a prestigious organisation. I wanted this assignment. In a moment of superstition, I had picked up that shawl, believing that it would somehow connect me to my mum: my good luck charm, my secret weapon, my comfort blanket, my passport to success.

The client appeared and made his way towards me. I saw him smile warmly and then glance at my bag. His eyes briefly took in the shawl and it seemed as if something seismic shifted in him. His handshake was non-committal, his eye contact brief. In that moment I felt I knew that he had already decided – I was certainly not the coach for him. We politely played out the chemistry meeting. I was absolutely not communicating who I was, what I stood for, how I worked or what a bright, creative spark I was. I was unconvincing of my flexibility, spontaneity or intuitive talents. It was a complete waste of time. Of course, I don't know whether I am right, but it was my experience. There was such an irony in him having no sense of who I truly was as a coach, because I didn't offer it. I sensed the predictable regularity of the boring blue-and-white shawl had stopped him in his tracks and thrown me off mine. This maverick entrepreneur in his new environment would have been a brilliant match. I left the building feeling boring, bruised and bemused.

He called me a couple of days later and said: 'You are clearly a very experienced coach. I have been trying to put my finger on it but I can't. The chemistry just wasn't there. I've chosen a different coach.' I thanked him for his courtesy in feeding back and said: 'I had a sense that you would do that. I wish you increasing success for the future and I appreciate you taking the time to come back to me in person.'

What I wish they had told me:

Sometimes it's just not meant to be. Let it go.

What I wish I had asked:

What's your first impression of me?

Notes

1 FLOW is the word used to describe a 'state of peak performance' in the research conducted by Mihaly Csikszentmihalyi.
2 A chemistry session is a meeting to test the rapport and connection between the coach and client to ensure both are comfortable and can form a useful and productive working relationship.

Chapter 6

Freedom to choose

Actively taking responsibility for my part in the work and owning my destiny

Flowing

I have not done much associate work. I think this is partly because, when I set up on my own, I really wanted to be my own boss. I have never really been good at taking instruction from others; even in my earlier career an instruction would appear more as an invitation to play, create and enhance than as a direct request. So, the chances of me finding an 'employer' who had the same view of work instruction was likely to be a tall order.

I can recall being invited to become part of a coaching organisation. It had, and still has, a fabulous reputation and seemed to offer a lot of opportunities in and around coaching. I was courted quite heavily to join and did invest a lot of my time checking things out, experiencing what the company's services were and how the people operated. It was all good and really was a fantastic opportunity. There was one drawback: I was going to be working for the founder and he had very clear views on what should be done and how he wanted it done.

In my typical way, I started imagining how I would re-shape his plans, how I could improve them, broaden their reach, make them more than he had communicated to me. As my courtship continued, I began to notice how unwelcome many of my suggestions, ideas and comments were: how my potential new boss prickled at the thought of change or new things. I soon realised that this move was not a good one for me and, as importantly, for the founder of this business. I am sure our different hopes, ambitions and fears would have quickly started to undermine our relationship and potentially ruin it forever.

Backing out at the stage I did was also not going to be an easy task. A lot of time, resources and attention had been invested in me, and to any outsider it would have looked like we were finalising the deal, not being at the stage of deciding whether or not this was a goer.

Having choice is marvellous and having freedom to choose is a real privilege, but making a choice is sending a message; it is feedback and is as often positive as it is negative. I knew that telling him I was not going to join his organisation was going to hurt him. No matter how I dressed it up, I was telling him that his organisation was not what I wanted. It could only be personal because he was the founder; it was his business and he had made it what it was today. I knew that, no matter how objective I was in my explanation, no matter how professionally I delivered it, no matter how well intended my decision was, it would probably still be seen as a slap in the face.

I acknowledged this and owned it. I didn't shirk away from my choice, I embraced it, I made another choice – no matter how badly he took my choice, I would work hard to maintain a good relationship with him.

It took time and effort on my part to do that but I got there.

What I wish they had told me:

Choices can hurt people.

What I wish I had asked:

Are my choices really free?

Falling

I was working with an organisation that was young, dynamic and very male. It was expanding at a huge pace, as were the scope and responsibilities of the leadership team, and they were having to sprint to stand still.

I was asked to coach a newly promoted manager. He was experienced technically, but all his experience had been in organisations in a different sector, where the pace of change had been similar to that of rock erosion and jobs had been fairly clear in their lines of demarcation.

I was pleased to have the work and keen to follow my coaching process to ensure we worked consistently and thoroughly. When I had trained as a coach, I was always struck by the notion of having the 'paying' client's voice in the room, i.e. a representative of the organisation or the sponsor of the coaching.

I had typically run sponsor interview(s) on my own so I could get the sponsor to tell me the key messages and in an unguarded way. I also thought doing it this way meant I could better serve my client because I would come back with a clear message and expression of what success would look like.

In these meetings, I would typically introduce the purpose of it and also be clear that I would repeat back all that we discussed with my coaching client. This was my way of heading off any attempts to get me to collude with them, and it would serve as a way of having them self-censor. I did not want to be a broker of unsayable messages.

Before I got any of my introductions out, the sponsor launched straight in and said: 'Before you start, you need to know that he is just not intellectually up to the job. There is nothing you can do to change that or change my mind about it. I need to figure out if we can usefully deploy him in that role or if he just needs to go. And, you can't tell him that.'

I was so flabbergasted at what had just happened, I said nothing. As I gathered my thoughts, he continued to tell me all my client's weaknesses and short-comings.

After the meeting, I knew I had to decide about what I should do next. I was so overwhelmed with guilt and obligation, I decided to continue with the work. This was a bad choice.

My work was contaminated with unrepeated messages from the sponsor meeting, with the guilt I felt for not managing the meeting better and with pity for my client. Needless to say, the coaching work did not make the impact either of us had hoped for.

He did remain in the organisation for a while but I am not sure at what cost. Although I know we did some good work, the one thing I cannot kid myself about is that, at every point of that assignment, I was free to choose, I was just too scared to exercise it.

What I wish they had told me:

The cost of integrity goes beyond financial.

What I wish I had asked:

What do I do with unwanted information?

Flowing

Holding a non-directive space when coaching, and the discipline this demands, has strengthened my approach. Having said this, let me be clear: I am respectful of the many models and ways of coaching. There are varying approaches with respect to tools and techniques, their usefulness, validity and the way in which they are offered. I am also very mindful of the pitfalls and seductions of consulting while coaching. I notice that I am touching on the sensitivities in coaching and the delicate balance of roles. The contract between the coach and client is at the heart of this, its clarity and specificity: a clear goal and an agreed way of working together on that goal; measures of success that are explicit and mutually understood. It can also be useful to explore what happens if something isn't working in the coaching relationship. Equally, when an unwelcome methodology or an inaccurate assumption arises, how do the coach and client resolve this?

I met with a new client to test whether we were a good match. In that meeting we had explored his agenda and reasons for coaching. We had worked our way through the key areas for attention. We had talked about what the conditions for success might be and what we were both bringing to the alliance. However, when I left that first meeting, I had been very aware of how hard I had been working to demonstrate my skill and experience. I was more tired than usual. On the surface all the right words were being said but something wasn't OK. We had agreed five sessions. He had not previously had a coach, but needed one now. I sensed that he was not familiar with feeling out of his depth or vulnerable. He was struggling to establish himself in a new environment, which was an unusual occurrence for him. It was clear from his story that he was used to winning and the prospect of failure was unfamiliar and deeply unwelcome.

A feature of this first interaction was what I want to describe as his lack of charm. He was brusque and keen to get down to business. I am flexible and curious and usually relaxed with most clients. However, this behaviour from him triggered in me a desire to prove myself, to relate more deeply to him and to make it work. I wanted him to like me and to partner with me in a more useful way. We both wanted to do the work but there was a gap and it troubled me. On leaving him, we had a date in the diary and a commitment to hit the ground running. On the surface we were on track. I played the conversation over in my mind, repeatedly. The clue was in my having worked so hard and the feeling of wanting him to like me. This was a recipe for disaster at worst; at best it would be playing at coaching with only shallow gains. There was a high degree of probability that the coaching would lose momentum and he would drift away, unsatisfied and disappointed, avoiding my emails and calls. I could see that I was too desperately keen to make it work and I was taking on the responsibility for that. I had been rescuing the situation and in so doing I was keeping him tense, mistrustful and nervous at the likelihood of not achieving his most precious goals. This awareness was valuable and created the conditions for me to step back. I knew that I needed to do something differently. I felt more optimistic ahead of the first coaching session. I drove to his premises with a lighter heart than I had when I previously exited through the car park barrier.

He was formal and tense, and he gripped my hand a little too firmly. I was brief in my responses, which felt appropriate, and I was matching him well. I had chosen to focus on what was important, the outcomes that mattered to him. I knew my part on the journey and I was going to hold my ground. As we began he was sharp and irritated by some of my questions. He seemed uncomfortable and was again apparently resisting the process, trying to hook me into a distracting game – a game that might ultimately lead to failure of our partnership and its precious aspirations. It was my time to choose a new path and find my voice.

'I am noticing something. May I offer that in the service of your success?'

'Yes, of course.'

'I'm noticing that you sound irritated and you have stopped looking at me. When we last met I experienced you as brusque and tense. I am wondering whether that's relevant?'

'I didn't mean to be,' he said.

'I therefore assumed that potentially I might not be the best coach for you,' I continued.

'No, if I was rude I'm sorry. I'm not used to conversations like this. I do want to work with you.' He had softened and something had shifted.

'Well, how might we make that work then? We both have a responsibility to do so. I shall let go of trying to perform. What might you do?'

He stayed silent and seemed to go deeper inside, evaluating his reactions and seeking an answer.

'I shall stop being defensive and controlling; if I'm not open this will never work.' The tightness around his eyes smoothed and the compression of his lips eased. He smiled briefly and looked towards me. This was going to be a fresh start between us and one based on mutual respect.

What I wish they had told me:

Anger and fear come in many guises; be alert to your client's real needs.

What I wish I had asked:

Was this a game designed to distract us both from the real work?

Falling

I had noticed that, before driving into the premises of the organisation with which I was associated, I was feeling irritated and resentful. I had spent most of the journey, which was of a considerable length, mulling over the amount of time I spent involving myself in activities that were not connected to my client work. I was always on the phone. My younger son was forever coming into the study trying to get my attention, while I studiously ignored him. It felt as if I was addicted to that environment. I was relentlessly paying attention to the next initiative and opportunity while allowing the precious time with my children to slip by. I was often exhausted back then. Busy, busy, busy.

My health was increasingly compromised, I was suffering from recurring infections and setbacks. My skin tone was grey and my features drawn. My body didn't seem like my own, feeling bloated and lethargic. I was trying to stay fit and energised but there was some vital spark missing. I was unhappy when I arrived home at the end of a long week, and bored myself with my moaning and wailing about the latest issues and frustrations. I kept promising myself that I would get a better work–life balance. I knew it was neither a nourishing nor a nurturing time of my life. I seemed hell bent on burning myself out and scorching those I cared for along the way.

That there might be another way was eluding me.

As one wise colleague said, 'this isn't the only place you can do this'. It didn't matter; I kept ploughing on relentlessly. Earning money for my family was imperative. I was coaching my clients, focusing on them, but, on reflection, energetically I was not a great example. I was hardly a role model for making informed and purposeful choices. The irony was completely lost on me. No matter how many times I resolved to do things differently, the seduction of my way of working pulled me back into my old habits. I stayed and limped on, doing myself harm along the way. It took me far too long to realise that I was free to choose. I could put myself at the centre of my life and work.

I now know that any resentment I was feeling was a symptom of my own lack of care for myself. I could blame that organisation or personalities connected with it. However, fundamentally I had outgrown the system. I was ready to invest in myself. All I had to do was dream and believe in my own capabilities and experience. I could start afresh and build the portfolio lifestyle I secretly wanted, on my own terms. The fact that I had not was more a symptom of my fear and lack of self-worth. The energy I was expending being angry and ungracious needed to be harnessed and recycled to deliver a new possibility. It was a very long time coming, but eventually I did take the plunge. I've never looked back.

What I wished they had told me:

> If you are feeling resentful you've probably outgrown the system. Now use your energy wisely to create the life you want to be living.

What I wish I had asked:

> What specifically is stopping you being happy and satisfied?

Part 3

Integrating

Integrating

Chapter 7

Maturity

Stepping in with wisdom, focusing on being consciously competent

Flowing

'We need someone to volunteer please. Who would like to work with the coach? Thank you. Please come up. While they are getting settled, I shall brief you all on what is expected of you as you watch the demonstration.'

We were sitting together in a neat 'V' formation in front of a group of about 40 aspiring coaches. The volunteer client was to my right. There was a hint of trepidation behind her eyes and yet she had clearly made a commitment to take part and to do so in front of a room full of strangers. We adjusted our chairs, making ourselves as comfortable as possible. I am curious about our capacity to know what is optimal, when in the close company of others. We negotiated our space, distance, angle and safety. I enquired whether she had been coached before. She hadn't. I asked whether there was anything she needed from me given we were about to spend 10 minutes together, demonstrating the coaching process. I asked what I might do to put her more at ease. She was 'quite happy' and had a topic in mind. The briefing of the 'audience' was complete and we were ready to begin. I remember breathing out on a long breath and taking a moment to smile. I was looking at her, taking in her face and sensing her mood.

'Thank you very much for stepping up as the client for this demonstration.'

This was the polite preliminary to an imminent formal coaching conversation.

'It is obvious that we have a large audience and they will be paying attention to us. However, I want you to know that all my attention will be on you, because we are about to do important work. I invite you to notice that the rest of the group is utterly there and yet let them be curiously absent.'

I was acknowledging the unusual context for this conversation and emphasising that my priority was her. This mattered.

You might hear many sorts of voice tones in your imagination, as you read this; the best I can offer is that mine had clarity, warmth, confidence and compassion. I was speaking slowly yet purposefully. I was mindful of the duality of my role, coach to my client and a catalyst for learning for the gathering. I was open and acutely alert. My heart was beating a little faster than normal; adrenaline was inevitable when exposing myself to the scrutiny of others. Those people had come together with expectations of and investment in the process they were about to witness. I wanted to coach well and my client was my focus.

'My commitment is to work with you as your coach. Together we shall establish our contract for the way we work on whatever outcome you choose. Please remember that we have all committed to confidentiality here and for the content to stay in this room.'

I am going to maintain the confidentiality of that coaching conversation here, now, also.

I settled to listen to my client's priority and establish the specific goal with my polite but insistent questions in pursuit of greater clarity. I did not progress until she was expressing her outcome simply and with a motivation to achieve it. The clearer she was, the closer to achieving her goal she would be and the more resourceful she could be.

We made our contract for how we would work together and communicated commitment to what was working, and shared a willingness to speak out if something was not OK.

Stubbornness is something I value in myself: a capacity to stay with the process until we're both clear on a goal. Any hint of confusion in me, a lapse of my attention, or me floundering for words or using too many are all symptoms that the clarity of the goal might not be good enough. I was calibrating for the sparkle in her eyes and the lightness yet strength in her voice, the flush of motivation and the alignment in her body posture. I was tracking her gestures and noticing metaphors, and was curious about her words. As I paid attention there was warmth filling the upper reaches of my chest, which gave me confidence. I shared back that I noticed her enthusiasm and strength of voice. She smiled and nodded and agreed that was the goal she wanted.

As she then talked of what was troubling her, the vulnerability was evident. I was with her and yet separate. I trusted us both to meet in the space in between. We followed the thread of her mind unfolding as she crafted her course and consequences. There were moments of deep sensitivity as I acknowledged what I was witnessing from her.

She seemed touched and relieved for her journey to be respected. I could feel the tingling in my fingers and the catch of my breath as we moved to the next step.

Freedom was flowing. She was finding ways forward. I said very little, a prompt, a nod. She knew her way and I was acutely aware of honouring that, with simplicity.

It is strange and wonderful what can be achieved in a very short slice of time: moments when the clock stops. Everything is held. The wonder of discovery is trembling in the bubble that protects and exposes a woman as she takes one significant step closer to her deepest self – all this witnessed by the learners who sometimes stopped breathing.

What I wish they had told me:

> Take nothing for granted; connection is a gift for all human beings, it is precious and magical. Be wise and tread carefully.

What I wish I had asked:

> How can I create such moments with the ones I love in my life?

Falling

It was a very early start and it was dark and cold outside. The central heating hadn't kicked in and it was a struggle to drag myself out of bed. I was going to meet a client, for the third time, and that client was a good two hours' drive away. There is usually great comfort in that first hot drink, for me hot water with lemon, a ritual I had copied from my grandmother. I didn't want to go out. I was sluggish and morose and the hot drink wasn't weaving its magic. It would have been easy to hang my disquiet on the hook of winter. Yet, the day before I had arisen just as early with a glad heart and eager anticipation of the conversation I would have with my client. Not today's client. It just didn't feel right.

What sort of not right?

Well I felt irritated and horrible, with a bitter sort of dread. I was nervous, like the first day at a new school. I found myself shouting at the radio presenter as my husband said: 'There's not enough room in this bedroom for the two of us and that high horse!' Maybe I wasn't going to have a good day? I suppose that was a place to vent my anger and I hadn't even known I was angry. The shower didn't give me that zing, the shower gel wasn't as foamy and my hair felt coarse. I noticed the grime where the floor tiles met the vertical ones. The spider's web glistened and waved in the draught. There was a dirty mark on the rug and the basin was grim with soap scum. This was hardly an enchanting start to my day.

I wasn't enjoying the coaching and that took some admitting. In fact, I was dreading it. The sessions had gone OK, nothing sparkling. I thought

I was very aware of the patterns he was displaying and wrestling with. I didn't know the answers but I could make a good guess. He was one of a wealth of clients for me at that time. Somehow there was disquiet in me and I didn't want to meet him. What was it?

This was very worrying. I was certainly not at my best and it did not feel good or fair to either of us. I had the script, I knew the routine and I'd had loads of practice at coaching. This must just be one of those things! Of course, I was capable of working with him! I was very experienced! There was an indignant departure and then an equally indignant arrival at the client's premises. Now the misgivings kicked in; I was heavy in my heart and this slowed my steps and stooped my shoulders.

As I sat in reception I started to notice how the staff came into the building. I was watching and listening to the way they talked, or not. I was suddenly picking up on the process of getting into this company and reflecting on what it might be like to work there. There were very few 'good mornings' shared. I could sense the dense atmosphere and the disquiet. I have no idea how these things work but I seemed to have absorbed the energies and frustrations of the culture into which I was delivering. It wasn't about the client, but it was about the system of his place of work, and how this impacted his welfare and his team and colleagues. There was a tremendous release as I realised this. I reset my state of mind and my way of being. There was a new way of approaching this client with gladness, compassion and professional integrity. I could be that positive parallel.[1]

I was able to work far more productively with him once I had noticed what I was picking up. I took this unusual happening to my coach supervisor to explore how the personal for me was impacting the professional in me. Realising that this environment did indeed remind me, at a deep level, of the saddest, most bereft and angry time in my life came in my supervision session. Mapping out the system of that company and setting out my boundaries was invaluable. It was important for me to be objectively in the present, with all my skills and awareness made available in the service of my client. Cleaning up my state of being as a coach was a significant learning and I'm grateful.

What I wish they had told me:

> Paying close attention to the client means that I am more fully aware of many more things that are relevant and have impact.

What I wish I had asked:

> How will I know when the reaction I am feeling is not just about me but belongs elsewhere?

Flowing

A dormant client got in touch with me out of the blue. I was thrilled she had called me and I was delighted that our relationship had weathered the passing of time.

Her organisation had been through a big re-organisation and they had a new leadership structure that had been populated with a number of new leaders. To help these people hit the ground running, she had spent time understanding the opportunities they could leverage and the challenges they anticipated. Having explored development needs, she then suggested they take on a coach. I was asked to have a chemistry session with one of the trickier characters in this new leadership group because she was very keen that he had a plan of action and support to implement it successfully.

This client's trickiness was evident from the outset – just setting up a meeting time with him was hard work. We finally got something fixed up and met.

As a potential client, I liked him. He was a little bit quirky; he knew his own mind and was passionate about doing his job well. It was clear that he needed to enrol people, get them on side and engaged in his vision, and that this would take a lot of effort on his part in both time and style. He was clearly doing something right because he had secured the job, against competition, and he had a mandate for change.

Our agenda for the chemistry meeting was unremarkable; it covered all the bases one would expect. What was obvious to me was that coaching was not what this man needed. He had a plan, a very clear plan, which was well thought through, realistic and achievable – it ticked all the letters in the SMART[2] acronym. He also had a plan of engagement. He knew who his key stakeholders were, what their positions were, how he could attempt to positively influence them and/or negate their concerns. He was clear about what he needed to do to deliver the plan, what behaviours he might need to deploy and what might derail him in his best attempts.

When I asked him what he wanted to get from being coached, he was stumped for an answer – as was I. It was clear that, at this point in time, he did not need coaching. This was my crucible moment: did I fish for work or did I make the right choice and decline to work with him?

He asked me what I thought he could be coached on and, before I answered, I asked him what his other potential coaches had said. One had apparently waxed lyrical about how they would explore the coaching agenda in the first session and she was sure they would come up with something and agree success measures. Another had suggested they could meet and review what of his plan he had delivered.

He looked expectantly at me and said, 'So, what would you recommend I be coached on?'

'I wouldn't,' I said. He looked rather taken aback and slightly crestfallen. I moved in quickly to give him the intent behind my answer. I explained that, based on what he had told me, it sounded as if he was in a fabulous place to crack on. He had a clear plan of what he wanted to do, a plan of how to execute it and an awareness of how he needed to behave to deliver it all.

He still looked crestfallen: 'But I have so enjoyed our conversation.'

'And I have too; it has been great to hear you share your plans, and it has been a conversation, not a coaching session.'

I went on to explain that, in my experience, not everyone or every situation is coachable and, although he was up for being coached, he really did not have a clear coaching need and I would not be acting with integrity if I tried to win work that wasn't there. I was quick to say that I would be very clear in my report back to the client that I did not think I could add significant value to him through my work, and that I would leave her in no doubt that it was me, not him, that informed my decision to withdraw.

The relief on his face took me by surprise. He was so relieved at what I had said because it had helped him find his choice. 'I cannot thank you enough for your honesty', he said. 'The other coaches seemed so sure that I needed coaching and as I had been sent by HR to meet them, I didn't want to rock the boat. I have already decided I wasn't going to work with either of them but thought I should at least finish the process my HR person has set up so I can legitimately say I didn't think any of the coaches could help me. Your honesty has given me great comfort that I am making the right decision.'

What I wish they had told me:

> Don't forget that making a choice sends a message, so manage the message.

What I wish I had asked:

> What are the real choices a client has?

Falling

Batman and Robin, Del Boy and Rodney, Ginger and Fred – whatever your favourite dynamic duo, my client and I were them. On paper, we were a match made in heaven. He was bright, enthusiastic and keen to learn so I was delighted to work with him. There were some things I noticed that he provoked in me. He spoke with a posh accent, very 'BBC World Service', dressed a little eccentrically, and reminded me a lot of the Harry Enfield character, Tim, nice-but-dim. I was aware of this but didn't pay enough attention to it. Our work together was fruitful and he seemed to gain a lot of value from our sessions. He was studious, hard-working and diligent, so I was always confident that he would complete the actions he came up with and come back to the following session with reflections on his successes and failures.

I took our work to supervision and noticed the deep sense of shame I felt when I started to talk about him. I laughed. It was the sort of laugh-ter you did as a teenager: scoffing and disrespectful. My group raised eyebrows at my description of him and I felt shame and embarrassment that I had shown such an ugly side to my character to this group of people. Rather than be brave and continue to explore this side of me, understand what it meant, how to embrace it and take value from it, I shut it down. I dismissed this part of me and held it out as anathema, something that is not part of me, an alien body in my personality that should be expunged. My rebuttal of this part of me was complete – or so I kidded myself.

We had come to the end of our allocated number of sessions and agreed there was still more work to be done. Based on our previous experience of working together, we agreed a new contract, which included ensuring we had a private place to meet. We had experimented with hotel lobbies, museums and cafes, but I always came back to how uncomfortable I felt, unable to be able to fully step into the work, and restricting myself in the tools and techniques with which I was prepared to engage. We agreed that we needed to have a room and he made the arrangements for this for our next set of sessions.

We continued our work together and he carried on making good pro-gress on his objectives. I started to consciously notice that I was judging his progress. Was it enough? Was it a stretch? Was this actually that dif-ficult? My little scoffing gremlin reappeared. I saw it, I knew it was there and that I needed to give it attention, but, as soon as I drew breath to speak about it at supervision, I backed off. I didn't want to expose myself again;

I was ashamed of this gremlin, it was so ugly, so hateful and I didn't want to admit to it, let alone own it and work on it with witnesses.

Needless to say, this little gremlin repeatedly turned up at our sessions. I feel confident my client sensed it too. At times, his demeanour would change when it appeared and he would make himself smaller, physically. The tone of his voice would change and lose authority. His normal buoyant confidence would start to sink and his eyes would flit around the room looking for something safe to lock onto.

I wasn't always consciously conscious of the gremlin in the room at the time but recognised afterwards what had been at play.

I have since realised that conscious competence is not an inactive state; it requires action and, if this state is the force of good, it needs to have positive intent and honest action. I kidded myself that being aware of something and just boxing it off was good enough but I knew, deep down, if I were honest with myself, that I avoided an opportunity to spare my blushes. In doing so, I sold myself out.

What I wish they had told me:

> Knowing is the easy part; doing something about it is where the real work is.

What I wish I had asked:

> How do I keep myself real?

Notes

1 Positive parallel is a positive construct that can be role modelled with the other person to enable a shift in the system. See Part 5: Themes and theories. Chapter 13 – Supervision triangle incorporating parallel process.
2 SMART is an acronym from Doran (1981) for a way of writing management goals and objectives. It stands for Specific, Measurable, Assignable, Realistic, Time-related.

References

Doran, G. T. (1981) 'There's a S.M.A.R.T. Way to Write Managements' Goals and Objectives.' *Management Review*, 70, 35–36.

Dörnyei, Z. (2001) *Motivational Strategies in the Language Classroom*. Cambridge: Cambridge Language Teaching Library.

Chapter 8

Peak

Having effortless access to my whole self as coach

Flowing

I have been working as a team coach for the last 20 years, which has meant evolving ways of working with trusted colleagues. In noticing patterns for exceptional achievement and then enabling significant conversations, transformative work has taken place. Acknowledging the journey of the team, establishing clear outcomes and increasing their systemic awareness of what needs to happen have meant that I have been involved in many satisfying interventions.

I tend to be more introverted. This is characterised by my preference for recharging my batteries with quiet time alone or by having a deep conversation with a trusted other person, although I would say that I am socially very confident and open to chatting with several random people in the course of a cocktail party or evening get together. I was always struck by the thought that, when asking questions of others and then listening attentively to the answers, one is assumed to be charming. What a magical formula for a coach! I also seem to recall an apocryphal story about the Queen Mother who mostly said 'lovely' in a range of voice tones depending on the circumstance. Many people thought, on meeting Her Royal Highness, that she was wonderful. Of course, this could be my imagination running riot, I really don't know.

What is caught up in all of this is, I suppose, my tendency to feel more tired after a piece of team work. Too much extroversion in complex contexts is exhausting for me, whereas I have typically found a coaching conversation invigorating, even with the most challenging of topics. Perhaps this has set up an assumption in me that I shall be worn out by the end of a team event.

Typically I used to anticipate the challenge of team work by being alert and a little prickly the evening before. I was thorough in my internal preparation and personal state management but anxious if there was a problem with the venue or service. Assignments were interesting, challenging and ultimately rewarding, but they came at a cost. Effort and application were required.

I had been paying a lot of attention to my group coaching work in the sessions with my supervisor. This began to effect a shift as I understood the meaning I was making of the work. Accepting that I was not responsible for the outcome was liberating, although I was certainly responsible for enabling the process. I had started to map the approaches that I treasured from my one-to-one coaching on to my work with teams. I understood that working with a team is like being with one body of many parts. I was adamant that it was not OK to walk away from a team feeling that I was fine with eight out of ten of them. There would always be a couple who were 'difficult'. Instead I found a way of noticing what shone in each individual and connecting with that. I developed a capability for remembering everyone's name, after hearing it twice, even in large groups. This honoured my desire to accept each person as unique and valuable, regardless of their behaviour or attitude. I began to feel naturally welcoming and I became diligent about setting up the contract and clarifying expectations for all parties. I developed rigour in my time keeping throughout the days and in the articulation of ground rules. It was my aim to work with the lightest touch for deepest effect. I believed that I could say whatever I wanted to say in a way that could be heard, and that it would be used to good effect. I finally came to know that I was more than good enough and could truly enjoy the journey of the team from start to finish. I valued my part in that. I was stimulated to develop the processes, using my own creativity. I was confident in following the team's threads and being guided by their priorities and thinking. I was relaxed around their behaviours and unfazed by tensions or conflicts. This work could be safe for me and for them. It was certainly worthwhile; finally I felt secure in the knowledge that I added value.

What I wish they had told me:

> There is a delicate balance between being aware of oneself and paying attention to the needs of others. Every individual wants to feel valued, even if it doesn't always seem that way.

What I wish I had asked:

> How can I prepare well without being moody with my family?

Falling

I believed in, trusted and valued my client. I had been working with her for a while, in phases, as necessary. This was in line with her career and business progress, her evolution as a leader and the responses of the stakeholders around her. Her work rate was impressively relentless. She was driven, talented, creative and highly intelligent. I had a great deal of respect for her and knew I was respected in return. She had accelerated her journey during her coaching with me and seemed to be flying.

As I look back I remember noticing, at a certain moment in time, how central to her venture she seemed to be. All roads led to her and everyone wanted a piece of her. I felt that her core was under threat and I had concerns for her health. She would express the intention of meeting with me and then several times sessions would be cancelled with different periods of notice. I was sensitive to the entrepreneurial nature of her venture and was more lenient about the cancellation terms, taking into account my perceptions of the pressures on her. As I write this I notice and question whether I was drifting too close to the client. Maybe I was overstepping the mark, losing my objectivity. Eventually we did get together and I found a way of letting her know my concerns. Again, perhaps I was pushing my agenda rather than hers. I knew, ethically that I had to express concern for her welfare, but I took the further step of suggesting she focus on this in the next session. The next session never happened.

I now imagine that she was paying attention to the progress or struggles of her business, which distracted her from paying attention to herself. The voice in my head now has a judgemental tone. I resented that she wasn't asking me to continue the journey with her. After all, I was a brilliant coach, with great experience and I knew a lot of things. I was exactly what she needed, if only she would get in touch. At least I can say that I had the humility to let her choose and I did not chase her.

My husband had been away working and I was very tired; I had been holding the fort, and yet fully available for my clients and my family. The pace had been relentless and I was desperate for some time away. My husband asked whether I would like to take some leave and join him. This was exactly what I needed. 'Yes!' I was busy preparing for my departure, packing, making back-up arrangements and fitting in the last things on my 'to do' list. It was Saturday evening and I received a text. 'I need to speak to you, are you free?' She was reaching out. I whirled into a conflict; if I did not speak to her now I would be away from very early the next day. If I ignored her request that wasn't respectful. If I agreed to talk what was

I getting myself into? What was going on that meant she was contacting me on a Saturday night? Maybe she had finally come to her senses and realised that I was a great resource for her? I HAD to talk to her!

I am squirming here in my chair, feeling the shame of indulging my pride. It was such a sad day for us both. I was eager to hear what was going on for her and I deeply regret that there was almost an 'I told you so' hint in my voice. I was not very patient and admit to feeling exhausted, overwhelmed and rather resentful. I offered to make time for a real coaching conversation once I had settled on my holiday. This session never took place. A deep black void opened up where our coaching relationship had once been. It was broken; the trust between us had been betrayed. The feelings of regret and remorse stayed with me, raw and sore for a long time. I felt powerless to make amends and indeed this did not feel appropriate; the chasm was too wide. We were over.

Supervision seems like the best route to travel in circumstances as challenging as these. I was, however, too mortified and disgusted with myself to bring it to a third party, no matter how much I valued my supervisor. Eventually, as the feelings receded, I found a way to raise this incident with my supervisor and there was a release and some learning. I grew through my reflections, but I hold this moment in my professional career as a powerful lesson. It is important for me to stay well, stay focused and stay with my feet on the ground, keeping arrogance where it belongs; it does not belong in me or in my coaching.

What I wish they had told me:

> It is very easy for us to become embroiled with ourselves as we stray too close to the client. That is the road to the deepest disappointment for all concerned.

What I wish I had asked:

> How do I recognise when my client is living my own challenges and then stay useful?

Flowing

When I was growing up, we had cats, Siamese cats. They were intriguing animals, and more like dogs than cats in their temperament and need for human company. The one thing that always struck me was how cruel they were when they hunted. We would frequently open our back door and find dead mice, voles and birds – a present from one of our cats. Occasionally, the cats would bring in what they had caught, not quite dead but damaged enough to stop it being able to make an escape. I remember the birds the most. The cats would nearly always break a wing so they couldn't fly off and, once they had finished playing with them, we would be left to sort out what came next. These poor birds were usually quite small, quite young and absolutely terrified. I always felt so sorry for them; they looked so fragile and so scared. Helping them get better was a challenge because you had to nurse them and feed them, knowing they were frightened beyond words. As they were so small, you also had to be careful not to handle them too much, primarily to make sure you didn't damage them further, but also to make sure that you didn't add to their stress. As we couldn't speak to them and reassure them through our words, the only way we could communicate with them was through our being. I had so much compassion for these little birds. They had been ravaged by our mighty hunters for sport (not even for food), and the intervention they had to endure to get well was probably as terrifying as the intervention that brought them to us in the first place. Our success rate was higher than our failure rate, and I like to think it was our being and our doing that made this happen.

I once worked with a client who immediately reminded me of one of those birds. She was small, young and looked absolutely terrified. Life had broken one of her wings and she was certainly unable to fly away. In our work together, I noticed that how I was being with her was as important as what I was doing with her. I felt huge compassion for her and brought this with me every time we met. I also had huge respect for her; she was bright, competent but stuck at this point and open to help from a number of different sources.

Her medical support was nursing her to good health and my role was to help nourish her. My experience with the birds reminded me I had to be careful with her, not handle her too much, not make the intervention to help her get to a better place as terrifying as the interventions that had brought her to me.

All the choices we made about how to work together were done carefully. We contracted thoroughly. In addition to the normal logistical pieces, we shared what we both needed to feel safe in this space, what our hopes and fears of working together were: examples of when we felt let down, dissatisfied, scared or happy.

We also thought carefully about where we would meet because the physical space had to feel safe. The place we met reminded me of the birds again. For the wounded birds, we had an old bright green Clarks' shoe box that we put them in. We filled it with soft cloths that had been washed in water without soap – we didn't want there to be any unpleasant scent for them – and we kept it in the utility room where there was plenty of sunshine and warmth.

Where I met my client had lots of light, warmth and sunshine, and she always seemed calm and relaxed there. She also had an air freshener that sprayed a fresh, neutral smell into the room, reminding me of the importance of scent as a contributor to atmosphere.

We agreed some objectives and spent a lot of time exploring current and past reality but, even then, I did very little. I recall listening to her, willing her to find use in our sessions, caring that she felt movement after we met, anything that would help her fly again. I really don't recall doing much with her but I did a lot of being with her. Now she is soaring and my little green Clarks' shoe box is empty.

What I wish they had told me:

Sometimes you have to be kind to be kind.

What I wish I had asked:

Does there need to be challenge in every coaching assignment?

Falling

I'm not sure how much I connected with this client when I first met her. She came across as quite fierce. She told me she was confident and competent but, even then, I wasn't sure whom she was trying to convince. She chose me to work with her and I had a sense that we could work well together.

It soon became apparent that the issues she presented were rarely the real issues she wanted or needed to work on. It would invariably take up a lot of the session time dancing around stuff, which left little time for us to work on the 'real' stuff.

I had a good sense that she needed time: time to trust me, to feel safe before she could get to some of the issues that were deeply personal to her and stopping her from moving on. Trying to pin her down was a real challenge for me. The session started to develop a pattern. She would come in chest puffed out, full of bravado and I knew that the next 30 minutes or so would involve me having to burst her bubble, grounding her in her reality so that she could access the 'real' stuff for us to focus on.

In supervision, I shared the pattern, the dance we got into, and I was reassured that it was important to respect the dance and let her get to where she needed to be, in her own time. However, I colluded with the dancing, encouraged it even, and found the steps got more indulgent, more elaborate, which took more time. She was easing into the coaching; she started to open up and in one session shared something big.

I was shocked, in a pleasant way. I could hardly believe we had reached a stage where we were getting into the 'real' stuff, that she trusted me with it and wanted to start working on this. It was a turning point for us both.

When we next met, she started the dance again but, what she didn't know was, I wanted to get to the good coaching stuff, not dance around once more. I was bored with it. We had got to some juicy stuff last time and I wanted to go back there again, not prance about with all this nonsense.

She saw this in me, sensed it from how I was being and, in that moment, I lost her.

I had lost touch with the human in the dance, the security the steps gave her to be able to engage with the coaching. The ritual of this pattern provided a security and a familiarity that had helped her eventually open up, and I killed it in one moment.

I wasn't overtly sacked; I was just told I wasn't needed anymore.

I wanted to self-flagellate. In fact, I wanted others to beat me and tell me what a horrible human being I was, that I shouldn't be allowed to coach. But they don't do that to you in supervision. My supervisor reconnected me with my being human; he connected me with guilt and shame in a way that could give me resources, rather than stop me, and he insisted I continue to coach because now I would surely be a better coach, connected to my whole self.

What I wish they had told me:

Shame, guilt and fear help shape whom you are as a coach, so embrace them.

What I wish I had asked:

Do clients ever forgive you?

Chapter 9

Purpose

Finding context, reconnecting with humility, understanding more than chasing success

Flowing

What's the work I want to be doing? What's the life I want to be living? What shall I leave behind?

These questions have come and gone and resurfaced at different times. They have led me to notice the work I love doing and to realise when the context, travel, complexity and style of work have influenced my choice to say 'No thank you'.

I have found myself increasingly enjoying coaching in the professional service firms (PSF) sector. These PSF assignments contrast starkly with the 'not-for-profit' opportunities that come my way. They both have purpose for me: one fulfils my intellectual curiosity, the need to think quickly, responding with authority and compassion while eliciting respect and reward. This coaching affirms who I am and how far I have come. The other connects with a purpose far beyond the room in which the coaching takes place. I then have a sense of being a catalyst for social, educational or global change, depending on the sphere of the charity and its reach.

I have been incredibly fortunate in the spread of sectors in which I have worked, the geographies to which I have been exposed and the cultures in which I have been immersed. The most systemic piece of work I have done touched 750 clients, with over 3,500 hours of coaching during an 8-year assignment. This involved working away at sea with officers and crew, for around 80 days a year. Members of the ship's company were my clients who came from India, Pakistan, the Philippines, eastern Europe, the UK, the USA and the Caribbean. This was a hierarchical and patriarchal environment, steeped in nautical history and culture. Many of the crew were away from their families for months at a time. They coped with separation from home and immersed themselves in the roles they had signed on for. They found ways of living and working together with a common purpose, which was the satisfaction of their passengers and the safety and integrity of the ship on its voyage.

I was extremely privileged to do this work and over time I began to notice how embedded the principles of coaching became. There was something in the way I was working that was rubbing off. I feel honoured to know that deepening confidence was emerging in some of the clients I met. They were making more informed choices, approaching their challenges with curiosity and taking decisions. There came a point when I would hear of banter between officers of 'You can tell you've been coached'. I even became a euphemism for respectful questioning, listening and enabling someone to find a way through the situation. I sensed that others found coaching and my approach one step too far.

It is essential that the Captain have ultimate authority, which goes with his enormous responsibility. Accepting this reality is for the safety and welfare of all. There are times when a coaching approach is not appropriate. Instructions must be given and expectations fulfilled. Having said that, a ship is a vessel full of people in close quarters and emotional intelligence is a very useful skill to deploy. Finding ways of getting along with shipmates and passengers is essential for professional longevity and peace of mind. My role was to enable those capabilities in any member of the ship's company who led a team. I believe that few people have had the opportunity to listen to more personal stories, with more care or attention, than I did. I had an impact on multiple outcomes which gradually joined up. I was welcomed, seen and valued. I hope that my clients also felt the same. Those preferring not to engage with me found ways of avoiding their appointments, which I fully understood.

There came a time when two planes were flown into the Twin Towers in Manhattan and the world was changed forever. This was devastating for so many. This also had a small but significant impact on my work. Budgets were reviewed in the aftermath of this terrible atrocity. My contract came to an end and it was time to accept that this coaching mission was over. I was saddened. This incredible opportunity disappeared. This work had a special purpose for me and it lives on in my heart. I shall never forget.

When I have revisited some of those ships I am remembered. It is curious when members of the crew say 'Hello!'. They are keen to tell me that they still have their coaching notes and certificates of attendance, many years later. I learned so much in their presence; there was good and poor practice from me but with the very best of intentions.

It is humbling to look back knowing how much I have benefitted from being with every one of them.

I also pay respect to the vision of the leaders who enabled such an initiative to flourish.

What I wish they had told me:

It isn't always comfortable or natural but, in the long term, a great strategic coaching initiative can be really worthwhile.

What I wish I had asked:

How do I say goodbye and let go when it is time to do so?

Falling

When I consider a time in my professional coaching life when I strayed from my purpose, I remember it with a poignant and exquisitely brittle sensation in the centre of my chest. It makes me feel sad and brings goosebumps to my skin. What a close call that phase turned out to be.

I was at a peak, work was flowing and the revenue was startlingly abundant. I loved the work and enjoyed my challenges, and I seemed to be set fair for a long time to come. I had evolved a model for a way of liberating exceptional achievement. I could draw it out, populate it with labels and sense when it was working well. Equally, it guided my thinking when there was a gap. I applied it to leadership groups, sometimes explicitly and at other times in my private analysis.

I was speaking with a friend about the possibilities embedded in the model. I was clearly reflecting and processing this for several weeks after. He had stimulated a vision in me for drawing together a group of individuals with a full complement of talents. If we all worked together then we could offer an end-to-end solution for an organisation's productivity. I put out an invitation for anyone who was interested to join me and explore what might work, together. Over time a group of individuals, with skills that touched every point of the 'Exceptional Achievement'[1] model came together. The discussions were turbulent, the way forward was often unclear and the emotions raw.

I found myself sharing my thinking, creativity, client base and funding with the group. I was increasingly focusing on making this commercial venture work. We became more and more corporate in our processes and ways of interacting.

Without noticing, my focus of attention had shifted away from being a good coach to trying to be a key leader in an enterprise of technology and strategy experts. The variety of personalities, experiences and values was challenging. We all dedicated significant commitment, time and energy to making something happen. To communicate anything was like addressing the United Nations. All media had to be deployed. Some expected PowerPoint, others bulleted emails, others a few paragraphs; some wanted a meeting together, others a quick or even a long chat on the phone. Texts and spreadsheets were in the mix too, as were graphics and photographs. Linear plans were desired or a systemic three-dimensional model would suffice. Until all methods, with translations, had been delivered, there was no consensus that anything had been fully communicated.

It had become complex and confusing. I lost my clarity. We weren't securing projects in sufficient numbers to keep everyone rewarded and it was frightening. My confidence ebbed away as did many other things. The more painful this became the more urgently I tried to make changes. I know that the other members of the venture felt pain, disappointment and deep concern. I lost friendships and security. I was diluting the essence of who I was and what was purposeful.

'Enough, stop!', I finally concluded. I was resentful, paranoid and bereft; things had to change. I realised that I was great when close to others but, fundamentally, I wanted to work alone, in a self-sufficient way. I most certainly did not want to be part of a team, let alone as one of the leaders. This was too much effort and came at far too great a cost for the person I wanted to be.

The enterprise was in some ways rapidly, and at the same time gradually, yet relentlessly, unpicked. I am certainly not proud of the aftermath and the voids that opened up. However, I stayed with the process, understanding that this was an important transition for all of us, which it certainly was for me.

A treasured colleague stayed the course with me and I shall be eternally grateful for his loyalty and generosity. He worked hard supporting every step that was taken, delivering his contribution regardless of personal cost and impact. Slowly I regained my equilibrium and fully engaged with coaching once more.

I have since held coaching at the centre of my professional contribution. I hear myself say: 'I'm a coach. I don't do strategy or facilitation. I'm not a consultant. A commitment to coaching is my full-time work.' This feels true and has helped me stay on track, on purpose.

What I wish they had told me:

> Diving into a 'good idea' before having clarity of what you want and whether you believe in it can be a painful process.

What I wish I had asked:

> What principles underpin the way I want to be working? How will this enhance me in my life?

Flowing

My *annus horribilis* was pretty horrible. My husband and I decided to have a Christmas at home, just the four of us. We had spent the last few years either hosting Christmas or visiting my parents in Scotland, and decided we wanted a change. We went out, a real treat not to have to cook the whole Christmas meal. I had agreed to call my parents when we got back from the meal but did not state a specific time. Therein lies a contracting issue and consequential differences in expectations. My father was very cross with me for not phoning home on Christmas day at the time they had thought I would (even though there was not an explicitly agreed time), and when I called later in the evening I got no reply.

He was mad, I knew he was and, every time I called over the next few days, I got no answer. I knew something was wrong, not my late call, something else – I could sense it, deeply. After a couple of weeks, I had an overwhelming feeling. I can't really describe it but it was overwhelming. I knew I had to call dad.

He answered. 'I was just about to call you; your mother has just been taken off in an ambulance. It's bad, she could hardly breathe.' I could hear the panic in his voice, the abject terror of what was happening to him.

We soon found out she had cancer; the primary was lung cancer but it had spread. She died roughly eight weeks after the diagnosis, two days after her sixty-eighth birthday. My feeling that the issue wasn't the issue was true.

She had a good death. When I say this to people, they look at me strangely. But she died at home, without pain (thanks to great care from the GP and the nursing team), and with a lot of her family at home with her.

Twelve weeks after that, Dad died.

He didn't give up after she died; quite the reverse, he was determined to live on. He made plans to visit me and his grandchildren, my brother and his wife, and do a load of things he had been thinking about doing for a while. His cancer was the slower burning one and, bizarrely, he had probably had it longer than mum had hers.

My dad would often say to me as a child 'death is part of life' and, as I have got older, that sentence has continued to grow and develop into various aspects of my life.

A number of friends and colleagues encouraged me to take a bit more time off, but my Dad's words would ring in my ears and I knew that I would miss out on valuable learning and contributing if I were to remove myself from my work for an extended time. So, I continued to work after mum and dad died but wanted to make sure that I took really good care of myself and that I was working safely with my clients.

My supervision was fantastic. I can recall at one session saying: 'No-one would bat an eyelid if I brought a case where I shared my self-doubt about what I was doing or confessed my concern about making a mistake or revealed my lack of competence about what to do next. The cases I want to bring are not about that. I think I am doing great work, I think my clients are being well attended to and I want to test that.'

I have long thought that supervision is not solely a remedial activity. It can, and in my opinion should, encompass all our work as coaches. Being supremely confident you are doing good work, thinking you are perfectly matched with your client and thinking that all is 'tickety-boo' are surely as fraught with blind spots as the reverse.

The death of my parents brought a new dimension to me; it allowed me to access endings in a deeper and more meaningful way. The importance of a 'good' ending with a client, and the consequences and dissatisfaction of a bad ending. Being able to spot 'deaths', 'endings' and 'loss' in my clients and their relationships at work also brought a new dimension to my way of being professionally. I can 'be' more with my clients, make space for them to explore loss and hold them compassionately in that space for as long as they want or need.

It also helped me hold the outcome of chemistry meetings differently. After the death of my parents, I suspect I mourned longer over 'what could have been' than I did about 'what had gone before'. This was a notion I applied in my work too and I became better at handling the quick death of a coaching assignment. In reflecting on this time, my father was absolutely right: death is part of life.

What I wish they had told me:

A happy coach is as effective or ineffective as a sad coach.

What I wish I had asked:

What other parts of my life do I unwittingly withhold from my work?

Falling

I have to think carefully about taking on development programme work because I often find myself feeling like the boy Cole Sear in the film 'The Sixth Sense', played by Haley Joel Osment. In the film, Cole confides in

Dr Malcolm Crowe, a psychologist (played by Bruce Willis) that he can see dead people. Throughout the film, this poor boy is continually visited by dead people and is terrified by this. Crowe suggests to Cole that he should ask them what they want, what is their unfinished business, because Cole might be able to help them. Reluctantly, the boy does this and his first attempt to help is with a girl called Kyra. She takes him to her funeral reception at her house and points to a box containing a video that shows her father had been poisoning her, proving she was a victim of Munchausen-by-proxy syndrome. Cole goes on to help more people.

When I am delivering a programme, I can't turn off being myself as coach. I bring all of me to my work and so 'be' and 'do' programme delivery.

I recall working with one group where I had an overwhelming experience of 'sixth sense'. I had walked into the room expecting to facilitate a number of different sessions and found myself looking at the participants but sensing a load of 'dead people' in the room. The sense was so strong, I actually had to step back because I felt as if I had been hit by a truck.

As the programme went on, I found it harder and harder to stay on point. I would find myself in a room with a small break-out group, talking about leadership stuff, but having to manage the overwhelming sense of fear, sadness and anger that filled the room. These feelings were also evident in the body language leakage, the facial gymnastics and the use of language used to communicate in the group. Like Cole, I was terrified.

The coach in me wanted to go there with people, do the real work, but that was not my mandate and my sponsoring client was clear that we were not to go there with people but, rather, stick with the programme.

I did try to do that but I could not un-know. The programme ran for a few days and I continued to struggle. In one of the exercises, everyone (including the facilitators) had to give feedback to each other on how they experienced them. This was excruciating for me because I could not be authentic, I could not share my experience of many of them because it would have been too much. I spent ages trying to dilute my words, find alternatives and de-sanitise the messages I had. I did well with some but with others I epically failed; they knew I saw their secrets, their shame and fear. As a result, they were scared of me, got angry with me, judged me and spoke about me to others in the group.

Every time I had to facilitate a session, my stomach churned. I had to run the session as planned and facilitate the group through a number of activities that uncovered more insight and learning for them. All the while, I couldn't stop feeling, sensing or knowing, and it nearly killed me to get through each session.

The whole dynamic was weird, warped and unspoken. I had not been able or, more to the point, was not allowed to connect to the real purpose in the room, so I did poor work and did it badly.

In my supervision group, I struggled and struggled to know what I could have done differently. How could I have managed that situation differently? I could see that the programme design was not strong enough to contain or work with the real issues that people brought with them. Instead, it gave them space to show up, haunt people, spook them and sit in the room like a spectre. There was a rip in me when I was with this group, and I wanted to pull the rip and separate myself from myself. In that moment, I wished I were someone else. My learning from this was actually quite simple: I need to make sure I contract better on purpose as I know I cannot un-know.

What I wish they had told me:

You are lucky that you get to know, so use it.

What I wish I had asked:

Does anyone else have a sixth sense?

Note

1 'Exceptional Achievement' is the name of Karen's original model – see the Introduction.

Part 4

Being

Chapter 10

Connecting

Honouring another, mindful of risk, deepening knowledge of self

Flowing

Over the years, I have demonstrated hundreds of coaching fishbowls as part of training people in coaching skills. I have a real love/hate relationship with them because I know I am working at the edge, in the moment, and that the success or failure of the fishbowl could turn on the smallest thing. To make these real, live and credible, I nearly always ask for a volunteer from the group with which I am working. Using actors or pre-briefed participants doesn't have the same spontaneity, reality or authenticity as inviting someone to join me.

In one group, I was working through a translator because few in the group spoke English. Having worked through translators before, I knew that the intent and meaning of some of my words would be lost in translation, and vice versa for the client. I also know that connection is more than language.

My invitation to this group was no different to how I normally do it. 'OK, if you were to get some top-class, free coaching for no longer than 20 minutes on a subject of your choosing, what would you want to be coached on? I suggest you pick something light, not your biggest or most personal issue but something you would feel comfortable talking about openly in front of the group.'

As ever, the feel of the room changes. Furtive glances go round the room, people no longer hold eye contact with me and I can feel some anxiety in my chest. Some side chats start and nervous giggles begin. I draw the group's attention to this and ask if anyone is feeling a flutter of anxiety; I point out that coaching clients often have that 'nervous butterflies' feeling in their stomach when they first meet a coach, just as they have. I carry on.

'Has anyone thought of some things they could talk about but don't want to raise them in the group?' Again nervous laughs and knowing looks.

'Have any of you said to yourselves, "I'll tell her this much but not all of it" or perhaps "I'll see how it goes and decide how much I'll reveal"?'. I tell the group this is normal. We all make choices about how vulnerable we are prepared to be with others, based on how safe we feel, what we think the other person will do with the knowledge we are about to give them, how much we trust the confidentiality of the other person, how much we trust ourselves, etc.

I give the group some time to think about my invitation.

At this point, I would normally go round the group and ask them to give me the headline of what they want to be coached on. I can select someone who has a topic that we can do something with for 20 minutes and that will allow me to demonstrate the GROW model.

Before I could do this, one chap bounced forwards and sat in the demonstration chair. He asked the translator to tell me that he wanted me to coach him. The other members of the group roared with laughter. Over the week, he had played the role of the jester of the group. He had stayed up late entertaining them all; he often cracked jokes in the sessions and was often the butt of jokes from others in the group. At first, I wasn't sure if he was joking with me or not, and my head started to tell me that I needed to make sure I did a good demo and he may not be the best person to help deliver that. But my instinct told me to go with it. When we started, others in the group were still laughing at him and cracking jokes, and some were incredulous that I was going to do a fishbowl with him.

I will never know what his intent was when we started the demo, but I was clear on mine. I would connect with this man with every fibre of my being, trust that he had good intent for sitting in the chair and see what came. As he started to speak, he told me that he had been having some existential doubts. The group roared with laughter. I didn't; I listened to that. He went on to say that this had left him wondering if this was it, this is life and then nothing afterwards. He said that this had led to him doing things he was not proud of. He partied too much, had an affair, drank too much and did not spend enough time with his family. His hurt and shame were raw in the room.

I held him in every way except physically.

The group had quietened a bit and they were becoming very engaged with what was unfolding.

Our connection was made.

The demo carried on for the allotted time and we worked beautifully together. The group were completely still and totally quiet. I could see that the translator was working hard and had a sense that he felt as if he were intruding each time he spoke.

In the debrief, the group were amazed that what seemed to them to be a joker trying to grab attention and make a mockery of a demo turned into a conversation they felt privileged to have witnessed. The lessons learned from this experience were way beyond those set out in the facilitator guide – the shift in the room was seismic.

I had connected solidly with my sense of self as coach and allowed that to guide me through this experience. I am not sure I have had this 'tested' in such extreme circumstances before and certainly not through a translator. The fishbowl is supposed to demonstrate GROW in action and ideally allow rapport and connection with the client to show up. The connection with the client was evident but the bigger connections are what made this such a powerful experience: my connection with self as coach – my stance of positive unconditional regard for my client, him feeling and trusting this, enabled a very powerful conversation to take place. The connection the group made with the power of coaching was significant. This revealed what would be required for them to do what they had witnessed (as client or coach). The group also connected with their potential as coaches, the possible difference they could make in their work and in their world. On reflection, I can see that this experience has been like a re-birth of coaching for me. It has re-connected me with one of the most basics aspects of coaching in such a powerful way that I have rediscovered my love of and belief in the power of coaching.

Not a bad result for 20 minutes of work.

What I wish they had told me:

> Good intent does not need to be translated.

What I wish I had asked:

> What happens when you consider risks?

Falling

Before meeting this client, the human resources (HR) sponsor had wanted to brief me so my antennae were up, ensuring I didn't collude with or negate what I was about to be told. I wanted to be open and receptive to the data I was about to be gifted.

The client was very successful in his job but his responsibilities had grown and he kept winning work that was getting close to drowning him. His organisation was worried for him; they were not yet worried about him because he was coping, but they were aware that his

Herculean efforts to keep things on track must be stretching him to capacity and this was not role modelling the sort of behaviour they wanted to promote.

In our work together, it became apparent that he was doing all the right things right. He had thought of and applied every trick in the book to make his situation better – this left me stuck. I have no doubt that my 'stuckness' mirrored his but it wasn't a great place to be.

In supervision, we landed on the notion that I needed to trust that he had picked me. I was very different in style, personality and approach from him and that maybe was what he wanted to access. I knew he had exhausted all avenues in his world so wondered if he needed to inhabit another's world to make any changes.

In sharing this with him, I unwittingly started the disconnect from ourselves and each other.

I have always prided myself in having a broad repertoire of coaching resources to draw upon and suggested that we try some of the more 'out there' techniques to see what we could access. He was irritated with every suggestion, then got irritated with me for naming it. The disconnection continued.

I lost myself as a coach. I got more stuck and felt more and more unworthy and wanting in his company.

In what turned to be our last session, I felt very exposed and therefore paid too much attention to my safety needs instead of the client in the room. To have truly served his needs, I should have told him what needed to be said. I notice that I spoke about it in supervision but didn't take it back to him – was this the equivalent of coaching gossiping? Moaning about a situation and feeling better for the moan but not actually doing anything useful to change the root cause.

The way I exposed my 'stuckness' was very half-hearted, I did not fully commit to it, which meant I couldn't fully access it and find utility within it to serve my client. Instead, I must have looked awkward, incompetent and useless. I can see now that not embracing this fully left me isolated from myself, from my client and from this organisation.

What I wish they had told me:

Moaning is not supervision.

What I wish I had asked:

Where do I look when I lose me?

Flowing

I had been flirting with the idea of training in coach supervision and coach mentoring for quite a long time – several years in fact. I had resisted diving in, even though I was thinking that this would be a sensible next step on my coaching journey. Indeed, I found myself saying 'I need to do the supervisor training'. This was a strong indicator that the time wasn't quite right. There is a world of difference, from what I have observed, between 'I need to' and 'I've decided to'. One is an aspiration that is well understood intellectually, compared with the other, which is a whole-body statement of commitment to act.

Gradually, on reflection, I felt open to a new way of being in service. This is very different from getting ready to learn something new. I am speaking of my own process. Supervision meant something to me in the grand scheme of how I wanted to make a difference. I felt I had put in the hours in my coaching practice and was finally open to the intensity of what might be involved. Several things had been resolved in my life with my mother. My husband was coming closer to retirement. My sons were forging ahead with their lives. This was my time.

In the interview with the trainer it was clear to me that this would be a very different discipline from the process of coaching. Supervision required an assertive and compassionate voice when working with that valued coaching colleague. I would also be holding a responsibility on behalf of our profession, with the ethics and reputation of coaching clearly prominent in my role. We would be highlighting the intellectual understanding of what was going on in coaching when the personal adversely impacted the professional. There would be learning mapped to the wider practice of the coach. This would increase the development of the coach. The wider system around the coach would be accounted for: the varied contexts, sponsors and line managers, stakeholders and peers. Supporting the welfare of the coach as well as their development would be fundamental to our mutual success. It would require precision and awareness with gentle discipline and care.

I committed to the programme and found myself in a room with eight other eager coaches who were ready to learn. We were all ages, from several countries with a range of experience and representative of most of the descriptors of the Myers–Briggs type indicator MBTI.[1] We were all women. I came to regard this as a group of fabulous, wonderful, fragile human beings who had the courage to grow yet again. We came together many times over the coming months. In connecting with these women, it became possible for me to notice my own contribution to the group, in a way I had never noticed before. It was life affirming for me. A mystery and a wonder gradually revealed with pain and joy.

The gathering of nine somehow made all this possible. I remember listening to a discussion about the impact of the coach's experience on the way we might supervise. I found myself waiting for the conversation to unfold and then adding my sense and intuition to the mix. I always had a voice and was happy to be a guinea-pig in the fishbowl (which rather mixes my metaphors)!

It didn't matter to me at this stage whether I was wrong or overly complicated, or should be ashamed. I felt comfortable to take whatever happened as valuable on my journey. I was also relaxed about voicing my vulnerabilities and concerns. I found myself noticing the complexities of emotions and responses in the group. I would regularly bear witness to what was present and acknowledge what had gone before. I would signpost what had been missed. I hoped to use my voice wisely and to see each individual. I'm sure that I succeeded sometimes and may have missed the mark at others. It was still worth speaking out. I was deftly straddling the chasm between 'thinking' and 'feeling', and I was recognising this capacity at last.

In a bigger group I would not have gained this benefit. I would have been much more guarded and overly attracted to a particular clique that would have felt familiar. There was nothing familiar about the mix of the women we were. I listened to their stories and their work, with heartfelt respect for what they were experiencing – the highs and the lows. I sought to be objective and discreet and to find the most useful boundaries for me. Sometimes it worked and sometimes it didn't but there was always something to be learned and to treasure. I may have felt frustrated or been judgemental or shown my prejudice on occasions. Certainly, at times these feelings and thoughts surfaced and then I consciously made a choice. I stayed curious and as 'OK'[2] as I could possibly be.

What I wish they had told me:

> Sometimes forcing yourself to do what seems obvious is not necessarily the wisest option.

What I wish I had asked:

> What is the most useful contribution I can make and how is that an expression of whom I'm becoming?

Falling

It was all set up, a practice exercise. We were on module two. I was going to supervise my peer in a triad. I was the supervisor, she was the coach and we had an observer. In addition, I would be monitored by one of the trainers on the coach supervision programme.

We all agreed to honour confidentiality in the room and specifically in the supervision conversations. I want to concentrate here on how I was experiencing my own performance. There is no-one else's content in this story.

I had my back to the door. I was facing my client, who was a coach. The wall was immediately to the right and the two observers were sitting to my left. In my psyche the right represents 'me doing my work', or my right hand is my 'doing' hand. As I recreate this now, stepping into those former feelings, that side of me felt boxed in, with nowhere to go. The door behind me represented the unknown threat, the unexpected intruder, the imposter. The observers to my left were homing in on the side of me that I associated with 'me being me' or 'who I am'. It all sounds very dramatic I know. I was on the verge of demonstrating my capability or showing how lacking I was. To be judged by peers is a challenge in itself. I wanted to do well but I was feeling quite strange.

I also had my client to consider and she was going to share her concerns and expose her flaws as a coach while reflecting on one of her challenging coaching conversations. We set out on our supervision journey. I was focusing on building rapport with her. I found myself sitting forward with my head on one side, chin jutting slightly, earnestly listening to her. The voice in my head was fairly hushed except when it commented, 'What can you say now? Well you weren't expecting that!'; I found myself settling into a rhythm of nodding, playing back and questioning.

'I heard you say . . .'

'I'm wondering what . . .'

'How will you?'

This process seemed to be delivering value for the client, but I had a nagging doubt. I couldn't work out how this was different from a coaching conversation. I was so well practised in my language and approach, as a coach that I was falling into the trap of doing more of the same. It turned out to be a good piece of coaching work, but we weren't there to deliver coaching. We were supposed to be examining this woman's professional work as a coach and to assist her in doing it better next time. I was busy coaching her. I even forgot this vital final question: 'How does this inform your wider practice?'

We finished the work in the time allocated and reflected on what had just happened. My heart was sinking; I felt a thudding in the centre of my chest. A headache was forming with a squeeze in my temples. I had a vague feeling of disappointment or was it just sadness? What I had become so proficient in, the coaching conversation, was not good enough here. The role was new, complicated and difficult.

'That was a coaching session,' said the trainer, with an intensity that made me freeze then focus. 'You know how to do this, so let go of coaching and concentrate on strengthening your supervision.' She gave me many more insights and some input and helped clarify the way forward. The bottom line was that I was de-skilled in the moment. I needed that directness to provoke my performance. The trainer had placed it well; that doesn't mean it didn't hurt. It was all part of coming together, to learn together, to be exposed, to commit with vigour to something new.

I resolved to work harder on the goal for the coach, remembering that supervision was all about the work. Firmly insisting on a well-formed supervision question from the coach would be beneficial. I would be alert for the key issue, embedded in the coach's story, which had got in the way of their good practice. I would support the coach in bringing to mind what was going on, by raising a model or theory that resonated for the coach to explain the situation on which they were reflecting. There would be learning, development and an improved way forward for the coach. They would be explicit about how this impacted their approach with other clients. I would be on the alert for moments when gentleness, acknowledgement and care would be helpful to the coach. If I was supervising, I was going to manage the session well and demonstrate good contracting and structure. Above all, this was my opportunity to be a positive force in concert with my coaching colleague. I would be enabling them to go back better prepared and stronger, with their voice clear and their confidence high.

What I wished they had told me:

> Supervision is complex, challenging and incredibly valuable for all parties.

What I wished I had asked:

> How do I work out whether I am hearing a coaching topic or one for supervision?

Notes

1 Myers–Briggs type indicator (MBTI) was constructed by Katharine Cook Briggs and her daughter Isabel Briggs Myers. It is a questionnaire for indicating psychological preferences of how people perceive the world around them and make decisions.
2 'OK' in this sense comes from the 'OK Corral' evolved by Franklin Ernst (1971) which is a diagram of the four life positions as set out in transactional analysis theory. 'Life Position' is a person's basic set of beliefs about their relative value in relating to others, which are used to justify decisions and behaviour.

Reference

Ernst, F. (1971) 'The OK Corral: The Grid for Get-on-with.' *Transactional Analysis Journal*, 1(4): 231–240.

Chapter 11

Threshold

Experiencing a time of terrifying choice, freezing or flying, knowing the potential for devastation or joy

Flowing

'Feel the fear and do it anyway' is not a motto that I live by. 'Feel the fear, pay attention to the fear, understand where it is coming from and what it is telling you, then decide if you should do it' is probably a more accurate motto but not so catchy.

Doing new things at work frequently scares me. I feel physically sick, and think I am unprepared, incompetent, exposed and not good enough. I am usually right; when I get scared I am usually all of those things.

The pattern that I notice about those moments is when I am being held as the one in the position of expert. My passion for learning and developing, self-reflection and curiosity about more and different situations disallows me from standing in the place of expert. Don't get me wrong; I know stuff and I can do stuff and I know there is always more or better or different or something – and that excites me. My problem is I hate how I feel when transitioning from conscious incompetence to conscious competence.

When I learn something new, I don't mind the initial feeling of being rubbish at it. I can cope with that failure because at least I am trying and, as it is new to me, I have no expectations of being immediately brilliant. It is when I reach that stage of knowing what I am meant to do and knowing that I can probably do it that I feel fear. I fear failing and the consequences that go with it; I worry about letting others down, making a fool of myself and looking stupid. That point of learning is excruciating for me because I fear I look, and am being, crap at what I am doing rather than looking like I am still learning. But, if I want to grow and develop, I have to go through this.

I am also aware that professionals don't really come with the green 'P' plates that tell others you are new at this. Most buyers will judge you as either good or bad at what you do. They don't really pay attention to where you are in your learning, how well integrated your skills, knowledge and experience are. But, professionals have to develop their professional practice on the job. No one does some training and comes out fully cooked. You need to practise, reflect, refine and hone your competence and confidence. At the same time, you need to give value to the client and project confidence that you are fit for purpose. This can be a bit tricky.

A colleague and I noticed that finding good supervision can be a challenge, particularly for new coaches. It is hard to know what you want, what good is, what to look for, how to decide, etc., so we decided to run some supervision tasters. Our intentions were to help coaches make informed decisions about supervision. We planned to run an experience of group supervision so those attending had a felt experience of how we supervise. This would be followed by a short presentation explaining the purposes of supervision (as we saw it) and points to consider when looking for supervision.

Although I had done my supervision training some time before, I was still developing my supervision practice. I had some lovely clients and was enjoying the work and learning a lot in doing so. I was at that painful stage of transitioning to being mostly consciously competent with a few trips back to conscious incompetence peppered here and there.

In the first taster we ran, my colleague ran the group supervision session and I did the presentation. That was fairly easy because I have done plenty of presentations in my time, I was in total control of the content and the delivery and I was confident I could do a good job. The session went swimmingly.

Then we got another supervision taster set up and it was my turn to run the first group supervision experience. I was terrified. The churning in the pit of my stomach was awful; I became incredibly self-conscious and overwhelmed.

In agreeing to run these sessions, my colleague and I knew that, if run well, the session could really chime for some people and they would love the process and format; we also knew it might not work for others. So, here I am, about to run my first taster session, feeling very scared and knowing that it might not work for some – and all that is meant to be OK.

For a second, I considered asking my colleague to run it. I know he would have done that for me and for the group so my 'chicken door' was ready. I caught myself and managed to acknowledge that this was my most hated learning state, and knew that the only way I could grow was to go for it and run the session, regardless of what happened.

So, I stepped into the roller coaster car, strapped myself in and off we went. The session was very like a roller coaster ride. Waiting for the group to respond to my questions was like those moments of absolute trepidation you feel when the roller coaster car is at the top of the long climb. You know it's about to shoot off but you don't know when or how deep the dive will be. We also had those joyous moments when the conversation in the group is going well and everyone is fully present. Just like when the roller coaster is on the flat straight and you can enjoy the moment, the point when you see people laughing and waving their hands in the air.

Then someone in the group started to share a personal story and the anxiety grew in me. Just like the long climb to the top of the drop, the creeping sense of not knowing what is going to happen, bracing yourself for the worst.

It was a good session. The group did have mixed feelings about the experience – just like a roller coaster ride. Some loved it and wanted to go again, others felt sick and wanted to go to the recovery room, and all of that was great. That is exactly what a roller coaster ride is like and it leaves you better informed about whether or not you want to go on one again or if perhaps the tea cup ride might be a better bet.

At the end of it, I felt exhausted and exhilarated. I was proud of myself for making the choice to go for it and knew I had grown as a result.

What I wish they had told me:

Every good coach has to wear green 'P' plates at some point.

What I wish I had asked:

Do I let this fear into other parts of my life?

Falling

'Dr Sam has a lovely ring to it. We might get upgrades on a plane', I joked with my husband. This was the precursor to me signing up to study a professional doctorate. Dr Sam has been in my sights for a very long time. There are a number of reasons it is important to me and these have changed and been shaped over the years. It has its roots in my 'stupid' chip on my shoulder. Dr is, after all, the ultimate badge to prove to myself that I must be clever! Although I won't deny that reason, which would be a stupid thing to do as it is still there, I can say with integrity it is not the only or main reason.

I want to be part of a coaching community that has integrity and profes-sionalism, where we can stand tall in our work and be proud of it. For that to happen, I believe we need to have an evidence base. We cannot justify our work only on the beliefs and assumptions of those who 'founded' our community, no matter how clever, wise or experienced they are. Any professional community benefits from evidence and research, and I wanted to be someone who helped build that evidence base.

I had completed my Masters in Coaching many years ago and still don't really know how I did it. I was working, had two children under the age of five, and was constantly battling my 'stupid' gremlin and the idiosyncrasies of academic research. But, I did do it and it is still one of the things I am most proud of.

Fast forward eight years and I decided to enrol in a professional Doctorate. I had a really good idea of what I wanted to research – my lack of respect of and irreverence for authority made that easy – and I enrolled. I can recall how excited I was, the anticipation, the confidence that I could do it; I had after all managed to do a professional Masters. I started well and completed the first part of process on time. Then it all started to go wrong. I had a change of supervisor which hit me hard. I really liked my original one and we seemed to have found a way of working together that really worked for me.

For those in the know, a Doctorate is a weird thing. It is a lonely experience that demands focus, confidence and tenacity. I thought I had all of those but I could almost watch my confidence flow out of me every time I started to try and work on my research proposal. I hated the feelings of inadequacy, of being so lost and so helpless. I did reach out for help but, on a Doctorate, there isn't really anyone there to 'teach' you.

One year passed and I had done nothing on my proposal. Another supervisor was allocated and another year passed and another, then another when I had done nothing.

It became clear that I was going to have to rethink this.

I have never thought of myself as anything other than a hugely resourceful person. People speak about being resilient or learning to be more resilient but this does not appeal to me much. I see resilience more in terms of coping with the hits: getting up after a full-blown punch in the face and standing square ready to take another one. I would prefer not to be hit at all, let alone a second time. I much prefer the idea of finding ways to dodge the punch, avoid the need for the punch, turn the punch into a tickle, anything other than get smacked over and over again.

My paralysis over my research proposal was a new experience for me. I can usually find a way or, if I can't do it myself, I will find someone who can help me or, even better, do it for me – I am resourceful after all.

Month after month I would look at my Doctorate papers and continue to feed my 'stupid' gremlin with Michelin-starred fodder.

One day I had to send a biography to a client and I noticed that I had the date I started my DProf listed on it. It was five years earlier. I was appalled. Not only was I stupid, I was also misleading people into thinking this was a real thing I was doing. If I were questioned on it I would have to say I had taken a break because I could not say, with any integrity, that I was pulling my research proposal together.

I knew I had to stop being half pregnant and commit one way or the other. I knew this, more than any of the other moments over the last five years, was the one I could not punt. I could not let another year pass.

I had reached the rock bottom with this; I knew I could not do it myself. I had not only failed to do it but did not even know how to begin to get myself in a position to try to succeed. Realising this level of angry helplessness was a new experience for me; I have never felt so resourceful-less – ever. As a coach, this has given me a new compassion for helplessness. I have always believed that there will be a way you can find; you make choices, decisions to change your situation and you can always change your situation, or so I thought. That had always been my experience.

I cried and cried about my impending admission of failure. I had let so many people down: my husband, my children, my clients, my community and of course myself. Although in that moment I made a choice that I knew would devastate me, I had mentally taken it – my fall.

My second epiphany from this moment was in noticing that this was still a choice. I was choosing to fail this; it was not beyond my influence and, knowing myself as I do, I knew I would allow this to haunt me forever and I did not want that. So, I quickly chose to take the path that had the potential to bring me joy. Dr Sam is back on the table.

What I wish they had told me:

Helplessness is not all bad; it can serve a very useful purpose.

What I wish I had asked:

Can you show me what good looks like?

Flowing

I was perched in bed, propped up with pillows, the duvet warming my legs and stomach. Still in my pyjamas I was ready to dial my supervisor.

It was a ritual for me to speak with her early. I love my bed. I've been saying that since I was a child. It is a precious place of safe withdrawal. I can lose myself there, enjoying being in my head. I explore the depths of my imagination in the vivid dreams that feature in my sleep. I remember so many of them. I was choosing to be in the best possible place for me, where I am in touch with my own deep self.

'Good morning!', I heard her say, in a very particular tone of warm command. She was eager and interested in my work. I respected and valued her enormously. We were colleagues on the call, yes and with very different roles.

'How would you like to spend our time?'

I had noticed a theme emerging where I had found myself focusing on the negatives, the problems, the issues, the challenges and the down sides. I was finding it really hard to put my attention anywhere else. I was feeling dislocated and lost. This was having a significant impact on my sense of self as a coach. I was feeling pessimistic. I had reflected that in some unspoken way I had kept my client stuck. We had colluded together to delude ourselves that her problem was very big and there wasn't a good way forward. For me, it was as if that coaching session typified the way my life seemed to be going too. I wasn't very proud of the way it was; I was very concerned.

We agreed to examine Karpman's Drama Triangle[1] as a way of under-standing my pattern and what had led me to walk so expertly into my client's shoes. It was hard to accept that I felt so drawn to the tragic story and had fallen into the trap of relating to my client as if she were me.

As I focused, a sense of my habit slowly emerged. I could see that I had taken on the tragic ending, like Snow White trapped in a glass box, condemned to a poisonous, frozen, dreamless sleep.

When things felt tough for me and I was full of foreboding I would slide down the path of despair, and no matter how hard I tried, it was going to end badly. There was no joy. My mother had been diagnosed with stage four breast cancer. I had been in shock. My supervisor helped me to understand that this was normal and that I needed to care for myself. It was important that I understood how my mother's diagnosis would impact me.

The strangest thing then happened.

I saw how the tragic scenario had pervaded my life story. I was aware of how my mum and dad regularly, not frequently, seemed to cycle around a loop of catastrophe. They picked themselves up with stoical determination, to set out on the same journey with a new set of players. This time, for mum, there would be no new journey.

I felt as if I was at the top of the highest vertical water slide. I was truly terrified of stepping off. I was about to find myself rushing down with the tips of my shoulder blades skimming the water, utterly out of control. This however is a story of 'Flowing'. At that moment I had a choice. I could be a doom-laden guide on the path to nowhere or, in this moment, in stepping off, I would face my fear of loss and tragedy. By choosing to let go, I was trusting that this terror would pass and I would find my own way. At the base of the slide there would be a deep pool full of drenching emotion, before I staggered into the shallows to clamber out and shake myself. There would be a rough towel that I would use to convince myself I was alive, with the vigorous rubbing on tender sodden skin.

I heard myself say, 'sadness doesn't live here anymore'. It wasn't a statement of denial; it was a rejection of a life sentence of sorrow. This created a space for joy in my heart and soul.

My mother was a precious being and I was deciding to be at my absolute best, open to all emotions, in the months that lay ahead. I would be with her at the hospital, I would lie next to her, we would laugh and cry. I would be joyful in the lighter moments shared and in the memories reminisced. It was going to hurt but I wanted to bring my whole self and honour her fully in her final days. My sister and I played our part as members of a high performing team. We contributed our capabilities in the service of our mum. As all was taken from her she never once complained. She talked of being afraid and in so doing she revealed, and I found, the beautiful woman she was always meant to be. This was wondrous for me, regardless of the frail, bald pixie she appeared to be at the very end of life.

How did this connect with my coaching? I had crossed a threshold and there was no going back. The intensity in my style lessened. A lighter spirit with a mischievous joyful bubbling core was prepared to sit with my clients, in their darkest moments, knowing that they too would find their way.

What I wished they had told me:

There is purpose in death for the living, for those left behind.

What I wish I had asked:

How does my parent's story manifest in my life? So, what do I want?

Falling

'We would like you to tender for this programme of work.'

There it was, the dichotomy. The internal conflict of 'I want to' and yet 'I can't do it'.

Except this was really complicated. Did I want the work anyway? There would be a lot of delivery, many coaching sessions, across a big population. It would be lucrative and potentially ease my cash-flow challenges.

There was something about the culture that was not attractive to me; it didn't feel like a partnership. It felt so much more like a supplier relationship, which didn't reflect the style and quality of the coaching work I wanted to engage in. I preferred to work seamlessly in a connection of equals. I wanted a respectful contract that would be so well understood that it would hardly need to be written down. I accept that in a business context it is wise to have a contract for the terms of service; however, I have had experience of this being a truly light touch document.

As soon as I heard the word 'tender', I heard 'please deliver this more cheaply'. I'm not sure that this was the organisation's intention. If I took a moment to stand in the client's shoes, they were attempting due diligence and seeking the most appropriate solution for their coaching needs. That is business. I was known to the organisation and it was, on the surface, a good opportunity.

The document arrived. It was 25 pages of questions, scenarios, background and proof. It demanded articulation of my philosophy and a detailed process to manage their expectations and the execution. Qualifications, accreditations, testimonials, supervision arrangements – the list was long. My heart sank. Time was tight and the deadline loomed. I wanted to be doing other things. I was angry at having to jump through hoops. I was resisting the system and questioning myself.

Deep inside I wanted to walk away. The location, style of work, quality of relationship and terms of delivery did not fit me. The context wasn't as interesting as many others in which I worked. There was a mismatch of values and when I paid attention I realised that I was holding my body tense, especially in my stomach just below my chest, whenever I walked through the doors.

I was so torn. Over the few nights that followed I was waking up after only a few hours of restless sleep. I was playing the words backwards and forwards. Round and round I whirled and I hadn't put finger to keyboard. In reality, I had all the evidence needed to secure the contract; I just wasn't getting started. I managed to convince myself that the work was desirable and I would be able to manage it perfectly professionally and it was worth doing. The fees loomed large in my rationale. I spoke to no one about this. I could clearly see the threshold; I just had to step through. Except it was the wrong door!

I wrote the required documentation, furnished the certificates and secured permissions from my former clients who were willing to support me in the process with recommendations. Once I started writing it was fairly easy and far less time-consuming than I had imagined. Except it was beckoning me across the wrong threshold and I should have walked away. I was too afraid to turn my back on the substantial fees. I was prepared to compromise far further than was good for me, for the sake of client volume and money.

As a new coach there is an imperative to launch one's coaching practice and get payment to return the investment made. As an experienced coach I do know that if I reject work, for well-thought-out reasons, then new and better work comes to me. That is my experience. Holding true with my path and my way of being becomes magnetic. I meet people who inspire me and for whom I am a good match, and the work flows. In valuing myself, I find others value me too.

On this occasion I chose to ignore my instincts and to put up with third best. Being with the clients in the room was a joy, but the interactions with the organisation were difficult for me. I now know I should have walked away and there would have been no shame in doing that. I would have been speaking my truth and caring for me, and in so doing creating a space for another coach who may well have integrated better and who then had the considerable benefit, in a context that worked for them.

One could say this sounds a little fanciful and maybe even self-righteous. It could be construed as ungrateful and lacking in pragmatism. What I prefer to notice is that over the years my work has flowed better, bringing clients whom I value greatly, and there is ease and joy in my work. Knowing myself and honouring the conditions that work for me is priceless.

Ultimately I had the conversation that said: 'Thank you for the opportunity; I have been able to do good work here. I have been thinking deeply about my future practice. I feel it is time for me to make space for others. I have refined my approach and am choosing to go in a very specific direction. I would like to close the contract.'

What I wish they had told me:

Sometimes you have to be brave and ask for what you want.

What I wish I had asked:

Who might help me think this through?

Note

1 For Drama Triangle refer to Part 5, Chapter 13.

References

Berne, E. (1966) *Games People Play: The Psychology of Human Relationships.* London: Penguin Life.

Choy, A. (1990) 'The Winner's Triangle.' *Transactional Analysis Journal*, 20: 40–46

Cochrane, H. and Newton, T. (2011) *Supervision for Coaches: A Guide to Thoughtful Work.* Ipswich: Supervision our Coaches Publishing.

Stewart, I. and Joines, V. (1987) *TA Today: A New Introduction to Transactional Analysis*. Nottingham, NC: Lifespace Publishing.

Chapter 12

Fulfilment

To offer the gift of being me for the greater good

Flowing

I seem to spend a lot of time angry. I quite like it because it gives me energy; it creates movement and traction, and feeds momentum.

For many years now, I have held a simmering resentment for the term 'coaching culture'. When I have heard it used, it is normally delivered in an evangelical fashion by a coaching fan determined to change the world through the gift of coaching. I can, of course, see this as a well-intended position but I also notice how much it upsets me. Systemically, it's offensive. There is often an inherent, and sometimes apparent, lack of acknowledgement from those speaking about a coaching culture, and this makes me mad.

I am a massive coaching fan; I think it is wonderful and I believe in the power and value of coaching, but not to the exclusion of every other form of business relationship or style of leadership.

When I was responsible for coaching at a global consumer goods company, I recall being in a room with a number of people from different parts of the coaching field. We were talking about various topics and someone suggested that we should be promoting a coaching culture in organisations. I flipped out. The anger that rose in me was so caustic it's a wonder it didn't melt my oesophagus. I was furious, enraged and struggling to contain it. The only way I thought I could manage my anger was to say nothing. At least, then, I could control my contribution and ensure I didn't offend anyone.

Sadly, that was short-lived. After many people made their points about this, all in agreement that it was a great idea, I blew.

'Can I offer a provocation?' I asked the group.

All eyes were on me and it was clear to everyone there that I was very emotionally charged. My heart felt like it was beating out of my chest and, my breathing was so strong in my throat, I wondered if I would be able to project my voice through it.

'If you insist that everyone in a business coaches their people, day in and day out, I believe you are creating an alternative tyrannical state.'

There was a hush in the room and a couple of laughs. I was encouraged to go on and explain what I meant. My words were spewing out of me like projectile vomit – I couldn't contain them. They sprayed round the room and hit people hard in the face. The venom behind them must have made the words sting when they hit. At the end of it, I felt pious. I had told those heathenish coaching amateurs exactly what was what. I had enlightened them as to the error of their ways and left them in no doubt that they did not know what they were talking about.

Nearly 20 years on, I have found a way to work more effectively with my pious anger: I write with Karen. I know that my anger is rooted in something worthy and, rather than using it as a club with which to beat people, make them feel wrong and embarrass them, I have found a way of working that enables me to offer my point in a productive and generous way that will be of benefit.

My anger about coaching culture got translated into an award-winning article called, 'Is a coaching culture an alternative tyranny?'. I have found that my anger needs and deserves a voice but a voice for good, benefit and improvement. Writing has allowed me to give to my professional colleagues and in a way that sits more comfortably with who I want to be when I grow up.

What I wish they had told me:

Your silence projects more anger than an angry contribution.

What I wish I had asked:

Can someone help me write?

Falling

The song, 'Do you wanna be in my gang?' rings in my head at times. As a Scot, I have a history of clans and I associate strongly with smaller groups of people. I am fiercely proud and protective of all the clans I have formed: my family, my supervision groups, my coaching groups, my friendship groups – all of them.

When a change to these is suggested, my antenna goes up and I become very primitive in my response.

Membership of my gang is precious. I don't ask anyone to be in my gang. If you are in one of my gangs, it is because you have been very consciously included and I value you, want you around, respect you and care about you. I do not give this to everyone. If you invite me to be in one of your gangs, I will take that request very seriously. I am honoured to be asked; I assume it is a very considered request and not something thrown out there without thought. This is clearly not how everyone thinks and, frequently, people invite me to join gangs or suggest potential members of my gangs without the same level of thought and care that I hold important.

I have often been asked by colleagues if I would meet a coach they have met at a conference or event as they thought they were a 'good guy'. This apparently insignificant request can send me into a very unattractive and unappealing state of exclusion. I have an automatic response to these requests that I often struggle to manage. At first, I want to simply refuse. How could they think that someone they have happened upon for a few minutes at a conference is right for my coaching group? Did they spend time understanding how they work, what value they bring as a coach? How they could benefit our group?

I then start to wonder if the recommending colleague really knows me and what I am about because, if they did, they would know that membership of my gang is a precious and considered thing. When in this state, I don't want to share anything. I don't want to share me or the magic of my gangs, and I hold on to that very, very tightly.

Over the years, I have met with many coaches who have been interested in joining my gang. Some have proven beyond doubt that I am right to be precious about membership, others have been brilliant and a fabulous addition, and some are in-between.

I have experimented with different approaches to manage this phenomenon. One approach was to make my colleagues hold on to more of the responsibility for creating the situation. I was clear that when I wanted more members I would let them know if I needed their help. Sadly, that one was mostly ignored or forgotten and the requests still came.

I then tried getting them to give me clarity on the exact purpose of the meeting. 'If I had a coffee with every coach I am asked to meet, I wouldn't have time to do anything else', was one of my standard sarcastic but true comments. The next approach related to time. 'How would you feel if I handed out an hour of your time for free to everyone I met in your line of work?' was another caustic retort intended to change behaviour.

I realise that I am the problem, not them. I am working hard to open myself up to the possibility of my gangs changing. I get glimpses that additions can add to the magic, not dilute it.

There is this side of me that is not generous, not free with myself, not giving – but it is also not at all fulfilling.

What I wish they had told me:

Find ways to express your good intent well.

What I wish I had asked:

Help me connect to my selflessness.

Flowing

'Would you consider conducting a webinar for our organisation? We want to support coaches and it would be great if you would offer your time?'

Well that was a first. A webinar: an opportunity to talk to the world of coaching from the comfort of my study; a chance to share wisdom and insight and to find my voice in a new way. I was delighted to have been asked and yet apprehensive about the way it might play out. I was not familiar with the technology and wanted to be sure I could deliver what was wanted. I had never put together a presentation for this medium and given I was expected to speak for 40 minutes and hold 20 minutes for any questions it was potentially rather daunting.

I found myself saying 'Yes, I'd be delighted'.

There was nothing for it but to prepare well. I knew that this was a moment for believing in the value I could bring. I had the capability to make it interesting and for the presentation to be worthwhile. I was surprised at how natural it felt to seize the opportunity of sharing my experience. I wanted this to stimulate each individual coach in an exploration of their own contributions. It seemed important to provoke and support the coaches to shine a light on their practice. It was also a way of helping them notice what was already working. I was excited, committed and sure of my purpose.

'Self-supervision for coaches' was the title of the session. It was designed to encourage self-reflection in a freeing framework, taking them a significant step beyond writing their journal.

I know that, previously, I would have been tense, at the mercy of my need to be perfect. The presentation would have taken many iterations, with the language refined, refreshed and removed. I would have dived into the bullet points and created pages of text with sterile, clean, crisp content. I would have been so concerned with getting it right that the heart and soul of the message would have been lost. My lack of belief in my right to be there would have dominated. The vulnerability that beckons when one shares ideas would have made me defensive and prickly, on the alert. By the time the evening came the strain would have been etched on my face and the frown between my eyebrows would have sunk deep into my forehead. My voice would have been the product of adrenaline and I would have created tension and concern in my audience. That was back there then. This was here and now and I had come a very long way in honouring myself.

I was clear on the central themes of the webinar. It was relevant to remember that some of those attending would watch the screen and others would listen to the content. The audience would all be remote. The session would be recorded and then shared online. I decided to keep the camera live on me throughout the presentation, even when I was sharing the screen with my slides.

Fortunately, one of my sons has a high degree of professional skill behind a camera. I had assisted him on several occasions and had even taken a lead role in one of his short films. He had filmed me up-close in high definition with all my facial flaws undeniably magnified. The dialogue and emotion behind the story were much more compelling than my vanity. I had to 'get over myself' because I was the vehicle for touching the audience. The chance to be filmed in this way was life affirming and deeply transforming for me, for my confidence and for my sense of self. It would certainly be useful preparation for this webinar. I was sure I could be natural and relatively relaxed while staring into the lens of the computer camera. After all, those attending deserved to find value; because they were committed to learning and open to examining their own challenges, this mattered to them. I wanted to be the best I could be, rather a cliché, yet accurate.

The internet is a great resource and I found photographs that illustrated the themes, complemented with some of my own shots. It was fun pulling my thoughts together. In standing in the shoes of the coaches I was considering the impact of this work and how it might land. In rehearsing the webinar a couple of times, the duration settled and I was looking forward to sharing. The technology was OK and, although I made a technical mistake on the night, it was really fine.

I was happy to be speaking with coaches, some of whom had dialled in from the Far East in the middle of their night. I wanted to offer a simple yet powerful framework for the coaches to reflect. It seemed to work. The pace of my speech was easy and moderate; my voice came from low in my body, which brought warmth. I wanted to smile. I felt relaxed and unattached to the outcome.

I trusted in my preparation, I trusted the audience and above all I trusted myself.

Twenty minutes of questions proved insufficient and we had to bring the session to a close with some unanswered. It seemed to be stimulating and to have resonated. This experience made me joyful, satisfied and fulfilled. It was worthwhile and I would do it again.

What I wish they had told me:

You are on a journey to become who you were always meant to be.

What I wish I had asked:

Why did I think that what I do is more important than who I am?

Falling

One day while sitting in a spa with my dear colleague, who is my cousin, he posed a provocative question. We were reflecting and celebrating all at the same time, indulging ourselves with some dedicated time to chill. Wrapped in dressing gowns and smelling of oils and herbal aromas we were oblivious of everyone else.

'How do you preserve the recipe for Grandma's apple pie?'

Sharing the same maternal grandmother, who was treasured by us both, I thought he was being nostalgic or cryptic or eccentric.

In my imagination I could smell the apples and the sweet moist short-crust pastry. I could see the kiss of gold on the top and the enamel pie plate nestling the base. My mouth was moist and my heart soared at the very prospect of a slice of grandma's apple pie. As a small child, I remember wondering what it would be like when she died and there would never be a taste like it again. Lost, not forgotten. I remembered the wedge of pie with its sticky comforting foundation, contrasting with the tart cooking apples and my grandma luring me with a large warm slice smothered in evaporated milk – the taste of home, love and being indulged. Grandma spoiled us because we were worth it and she offered food because it was the best way she knew how to give love.

So, having posed the question, my cousin made it clear to me that it would be such a shame if, after all those years of coaching, that my 'special recipe' passed with me. It sounds strange recalling it now, but he triggered a spark in me that took hold and spread through us both.

I became increasingly curious as to how I might harness my coaching experience in support of the wider coaching community. I could give back by offering both my knowledge and my noticing. How might I do that in a way that would add value to a much wider group? As one of my clients once said: 'How do you reach a bigger group of people, way beyond those whom you might touch directly in conversation?' I suppose that is how it started.

In one of my own coaching sessions I found myself tapping into the core of my body, spinning at my very centre, generating energy and origination. A model was born that would be a framework for exploring the themes and patterns I had noticed in my work at sea. I captured it and built on it and wrote the story of it. I tested the theory with colleagues and clients. I was exposed to encouraging feedback mixed with damning scepticism. My colleague and I kept going. We drew up a spreadsheet and his dear friend transitioned this into a dynamic entity. A kind and skilled client generously evolved a PowerPoint unfolding an animated version. It was tested and sense checked further. The logic, validity and relevance were examined by countless interested and resistant parties. We were not about to quit.

My cousin managed the programme of work that led to this tool being mounted online. It became a questionnaire designed to evaluate the work of a coach as they reflected on a coaching conversation. I have no idea how it morphed and emerged; we kept following the thread and held with the intention of sharing generously. The internet was new and beckoning, answering the question of how to reach that wider group, touching a community of interest, a place for our gift.

The tool was built, the offer was made and nobody visited. All our love and care and knowledge wrapped up in that framework were redundant. It felt like throwing a grand party for which one prepares for weeks and slowly but surely, despite reassurances to the contrary, on the night of the celebrations the doorbell stayed silent. It was as if we were left chatting distractedly with one or two stalwarts. We were trying to spread ourselves across the party landscape, which sadly and shamefacedly echoed with the sounds of hollow disappointment.

This feeling persisted for a very long time. We waited and held the faith, believing that it was a valuable contribution and the profession would evolve in need and purpose. The time would eventually come when it was of use and supported continuing professional development.[1] We were very patient.

What I wish they had told me:

> You can be so far ahead of the curve it can seem like a straight road to nowhere.

What I wish I had asked:

How might I be more resilient and trust my instincts, regardless of setbacks?

Note

1 Continuing professional development framework: me:my™coach – please refer to the Appendix.

Part 5

Themes and theories

Chapter 13

Themes and theories

In writing this book, we were struck by the number of applications the stories offered if viewed from different perspectives. In addition to the original intent of the book, we noticed how useful it had been for us to share these experiences in supervision, with our peers and, where appropriate, our clients. In doing so, our learning was leveraged, small details, points of little consequence and also big fat juicy points were harvested in our curiosity to learn, and enhanced our coaching capability and confidence.

We thought that readers at different stages of their journeys might find it useful for us to share some of the models, frameworks, theories, tools and techniques that enabled us to learn, grow and integrate our experiences into our practice.

There were a number of key themes that emerged, so we have focused on those rather than trying to cover every possible learning topic that could be gleaned from our stories. We are at pains to point out that the following is not an exhaustive list of models and theories that we use or that relate to our work. There are many more we could have included and applied with equal enthusiasm. In the course of writing the stories, a number of them could be viewed through a transactional analysis lens when trying to unwind the story, understand it and learn from it. It is also fair to say that the stories could be viewed through a number of different lenses – a systemic model, the seven-eyed model, gestalt models, etc. – to achieve equal understanding and learning. It just so happened that many of our stories sat neatly with TA. The following is intended to serve more as a reference for further reading and learning should you wish to take the stories to another, different and more technical level.

As there were some key themes, we have grouped them under the relevant theories and we have included full references in the Bibliography should you wish to read about them further.

As a result, the arrangement of this chapter is as follows:

Transactional analysis

(a) Drama Triangle
(b) Parent–Adult–Child (P-A-C) ego-state models
(c) Protection, permission and potency
(d) Working Styles
(e) Psychological Distance.

General

(a) Fundamental attribution error
(b) Chemistry: what does good look like?
(c) Contracting
(d) Flow
(e) Supervision Triangle incorporating parallel process
(f) The GROW model
(g) Competencies.

Transactional analysis

Transactional analysis, or simply TA, is a theory about the way people develop, communicate and change, in relation to themselves and others. It is a psychological approach and is used therapeutically. It has also been deployed in wider contexts, such as education, by social workers, in the probation service, and organisationally, including for management training. Wherever it seems important to understand individuals, how they relate to others and the way they communicate, TA provides valuable insights. It is highly useful and effective for reflecting and thinking about coaching practice and offers relevant theories for learning and development in coach supervision sessions.

TA was originally developed in the USA by the well-respected Psychiatrist Eric Berne in the 1950s. TA became known internationally through his many books. Berne founded the International Transactional Analysis Association, which has become the largest association and professional body for people interested in and practising TA.

Centrally, TA promotes self-respect and acceptance and is mutually respectful. It aspires to a state of autonomy for individuals. A state when an individual understands from where their behaviours are derived, can explore what is possible and can decide how to solve problems to change and behave in more successful ways.

Stewart and Joines (1987: 6) state that:

'TA is based on three philosophical assumptions:

1 That people are OK
2 That everyone has the capacity to think
3 That people decide their own destiny and they can change the decisions they make

TA has a theory of personality, a theory of communication, one of child development and also of psychopathology.'

TA has a range of models and frameworks that describe the psychological concepts in simple language. People generally find these models easy to relate to and practical in their application. The models could be misunderstood as shallow or superficial, when in fact there is depth and complexity behind the theories – which are profound.

Some of the models and theories are explored in the next section. They serve to propose and explain how behaviours and ways of communicating lead to consequences that are not necessarily desired outcomes. They enable insight, learning and development, and the opportunity to change how we experience ourselves and our relationships with others.

TA models offer ways of understanding 'What just happened?', 'Why did that client trigger me?', 'Why do I feel so awful as a consequence of that conversation?', 'Why do I get upset?' and 'What is stopping me?'. These are some of the questions that arise from our coaching stories. In sharing the theories, we hope that you find ways of deepening your awareness to make informed choices in your own coaching work.

(a) The Drama Triangle

In TA terms, there are times when psychological games arise. Eric Berne (1966) was the first to describe the predictable structure of these games. He devised ways of analysing the games. He refined his definition in his final book *What Do You Say After Hello?* Stewart and Joines (1987: 242–243) give a slightly less technical description from Berne's formula:

'A game is the process of doing something with an ulterior motive that:

1 Is outside Adult awareness
2 Does not become explicit until the participants switch the way they are behaving; and
3 Results in everyone feeling confused, misunderstood and wanting to blame the other person.'

Any such game will have purpose, even if it is associated with a feeling that is uncomfortable or painful. This is known as the negative pay-off. The outcome may seem familiar: 'I knew that would happen!' Or 'This always happens to me?' The consequence is surprising and holds dramatic energy, as a result of a shift in the interaction. This is strangely comforting because, once again, 'it is exactly what I expect'.

These games can happen when we are feeling vulnerable or disconnected in some way. Unable to deal with the deeper concern we engage in distracting, ineffective communication, which has poor consequences. At least being in contact with someone, even if painful, is better than being ignored and alone.

Karpman (1968) devised a powerful, elegant, yet simple, diagram to illustrate and analyse conflict. He set out the conflict roles and a way of illustrating how participants switch roles in the conflict. The switch of role leads to the negative pay-off or deeply uncomfortable feeling. There are three roles:

1   The Victim: this label is to illustrate someone who is not a victim but is acting out a role as if they are a victim. Their stance is 'poor me'. The role is characterised as helpless, hopeless or worthless, feeling unable to solve their problem or achieve insight. To achieve the pay-off the Victim will seek out either a Rescuer who will save the day and perpetuate the Victim's negative feelings or a Persecutor who will play the role to keep the Victim in a 'less than' position.

2   The Rescuer wants to 'help'. Their theme is either the hard worker ('look how hard I'm trying') or the caretaker ('I'm only trying to help!'). They feel guilty if they don't dive in and help. They also keep the Victim dependent, effectively giving the Victim permission to fail. When the Rescuer focuses on the Victim it is a distraction from their own concerns. The avoidance of the Rescuer's own problems is masked as worries for the needs of the Victim.

3   The Persecutor has a theme of blaming others ('It's all your fault') and they behave in a controlling, judgemental, self-righteous, inflexibly superior manner. They act during the drama in a way that puts other people down. This frustration distracts from their own vulnerability, fear or anger.

The Victim may focus their energy on switching roles with the persecutor or rescuer. Cochrane and Newton (2011: 45) explain: 'when the helpful Rescuer changes to helpless Victim, by feeling completely inadequate to the work in hand; while the other person's hopeless Victim switches to Persecutor "I thought you'd be more help than that!".'

The Victim who triggers and enables the criticism from the Persecutor may suddenly switch to rejection of the Persecutor: 'I'm off, I can't do this anymore!' The Persecutor then feels confused by that rejection, having no sense of 'what I've done to cause that'.

Stewart and Joines (1987: 236–237) highlight the discounting evident in each of the three roles:

> 'All games involve discounting:
>
> - The Persecutor discounts others' value or dignity
>
> - The Rescuer discounts others' abilities to think for themselves and act on their own initiative
>
> - A Victim discounts herself

If the Victim seeks out a Persecutor then he/she agrees with the Persecutor by viewing himself/herself as a person to be rejected and belittled. If the Victim is seeking the Rescuer, they believe that they need help to think, decide or act.'

In setting this out, these roles are following our scripts, which we learned in our early years. The spoken or implicit messages from parents or authority figures in our young lives lead us to take on beliefs about ourselves and others, which we then play out. Therefore, a game is not about the current reality but is replaying the theme which enables us to avoid experiencing our authentic feelings of joy, fear, sadness and anger. Games distract us from attending to our vulnerabilities and ensure that we avoid the anticipated pain of change and the fear of finding new ways of being. The transition to authenticity lies in recognising the underlying truth behind the behaviours in the game.

The truth is that people have problems and difficulties that they have not yet found ways of mitigating or solving, let alone voicing. People can help others without smothering or controlling, showing genuine concern, while believing in another's capacity to work it out for themselves. Being assertive and potent in saying what one can and can't do without punishing, accusing or blaming is also desirable.

The description above shows the possibility of giving recognition and contact with openness and respect, as illustrated in Acey Choy's (1990) 'Winner's Triangle'.

Potent behaviours of challenging usefully, setting boundaries and bringing structure in pursuit of a viable solution offer ways of declining game playing. Responsive behaviours of listening, nurturing and coaching enable the vulnerable person to voice their underlying issues and concerns. Giving oneself the space for being vulnerable and asking for what is needed and wanted, giving voice, is the antithesis of the Victim behaviour.

These winning behaviours have the capacity to restore mutual respect and enable productive communication. Understanding ourselves in relation to others and declining the game playing enable us to write new stories for ourselves about 'who we are' and 'how OK we are'. This potentially leads, step by step, to a healthier and more fulfilling sense of self.

I have found myself thrown by the consequences of engaging in a 'Drama Triangle' with some of my clients. It has been disorientating, painful and demeaning. I have grown many times from reflecting on these dynamics and, in conversation with my supervisor, have navigated increasing levels of skill – with voice.

(b)   Parent–Adult–Child (P-A-C) model

One of the models relating to the theory of personality is the ego-state model (Berne, 1966; Stewart and Joines, 1987). This suggests that we have internal experience, thoughts and feelings, of three distinct ego-states. We can change from Child to Parent to Adult processes many times a day. This is evidenced in our external behaviours, through our language and tone of voice, and also in our body language – posture, gestures, facial expressions, eye contact and breathing.

The **Parent** is characterised by behaviours, thinking and feeling copied from parents or other parent-like models, and I am said to be in my Parent ego-state. When I am thinking, behaving and responding to the real-time information that is around me, and I am using all the grown-up faculties and resources I have, I am said to be in my **Adult** ego-state.

The **Child** is characterised by feelings, thoughts and behaviours that were evident in me when I was a child, and I am said to be in my Child ego-state. We take mainly the content of our childhood experiences and we continue to evolve this into adulthood.

When in touch with feelings that relate to a particular ego-state, then I also exhibit consistent behaviours that also define that same ego-state, e.g. fear of being reprimanded might lead to heart racing, perspiration and panic, expressed in behaviours such as widening of the eyes, tense musculature, face touching, foot waggling. These are from the Child ego-state. This is usually represented by the structural state diagram.

Now consider how the ego-states are used, and what processes are evident; this is known as the functional ego-state model, which comprises positive and negative manifestations.

The positive expressions of these three ego-states are:

- Structuring Parent bringing clarity and boundaries
- Nurturing Parent offering understanding and encouragement
- Accounting Adult sharing facts formulated in the present
- Adapted Child behaving politely and considerately
- Free Child expressing creativity and spontaneity.

The negative manifestations of the ego-states:

- Critical Parent making judgements and finding fault
- Marshmallowing Parent inconsistently smothering and over-indulgent
- Compliant or resistant Child behaving in a sulking or rebellious fashion
- Immature Child appearing reckless or selfish.

It is important to remember that you always have a choice. When experiencing your own internal process, increase your awareness of 'which ego-state am I using?'. You can choose which ego-state you use in your communication and you do not have to be 'hooked' by others.

The positive behavioural ego-states set out above comprise what is also known as the 'Integrating Adult'. This is a healthy and highly functioning way of being and behaving, a wise expression of ourselves.

Choosing one of these ways of behaving will enable you to have more productive, less dramatic, less energy-sapping and emotionally destabilising interactions. Accounting is taking notice of the factual reality in the present, in an objective, clear manner.

To further illustrate how the ego-states play out consider the following.

When we communicate with another person the interactions that take place are called transactions in TA. This is a complex area for analysis and takes account of the evident behaviours and what is actually happening. There are also ulterior transactions that refer to the underlying messages, which can be psychologically powerful, and are about the 'real' intention and meaning in the exchange of communication and behaviour. I may be saying one thing, 'I am sure you can come up with something', and the ulterior message is 'but I don't believe you can'.

Examples of a range of transactions:

1   Critical parental behaviours are likely to trigger behaviours that are childish, resistant, rebellious, sulking or overly submissive. These Child ego-state behaviours may in turn frustrate and therefore

amplify the critical Parent ego-state, escalating the situation and creating a breakdown of communication and understanding, which seem lacking in mutual respect.

2   Spontaneous, playful Child ego-state behaviours might stimulate distraction and a similarly playful Child ego-state in the other person, leading to avoidance or failure to deliver a task.

3   Overly protective Parent ego-state behaviours are likely to provoke negative Child ego-state behaviours, which become disabling and block the person from finding their solutions.

4   An invitation to look at a problem and discuss finding a way forward, given the current facts, will be witnessed as an Adult–Adult interaction that is focused and calm, but alert.

In my work with clients I have fallen into the trap of moving into critical Parent, triggering a resistant Child ego-state behaviour in that client. This happened even when I was trying not to do so. The ulterior message crept in, outside of my conscious awareness. I left the session feeling disconcerted, frustrated and dissatisfied with the quality of my work. I noticed the feelings and took this concern to supervision. I reflected with the wise being my supervisor had proved to be, and I noticed that the client had triggered me. I fell into the trap of letting memories from my earlier personal life encroach on my professional practice. I gained awareness and developed a strategy to behave in a more Integrating Adult way at the next coaching session. I took this learning and mapped it across my professional coaching practice, and I endeavoured to be mindful the next time I met a person behaving like that.

(c) Protection, permission and potency

The TA writer Pat Crossman (1966) wrote of three conditions for therapeutic change: protection, permission and potency. When Claude Steiner and the late Eric Berne developed the theory of transactional analysis, they held a basic belief that people were 'born princes and princesses, until their parents turned them into frogs'. Steiner played an important role in the analysis of 'life scripts' that are developed at an early stage. Stewart and Joines (1987: 330) defined life script as 'an unconscious life-plan made in childhood, reinforced by parents, "justified" by subsequent events, and culminating in a chosen alternative'.

In order to move to a chosen alternative in coaching, the coach must set up the condition of protection. This condition is how, in our view, the coach works with the client to mitigate the risks inherent in change, making it seem safe, as the client finds new ways of behaving. The coach assists the client in thinking through how to manage the response of others and to feel good about the consequences of the change they choose. Structure and clarity support the process of protection.

Permission is the way in which the coach models and actively supports the client to change. The coach may do this verbally?: 'It's OK to feel what you feel.' They may also model permission in their own behaviour, arising from a principle of positive regard for the client, without judgement or censure. The coach may foster curiosity in the client and enable playful experimentation with possibilities. This affirms that the client is capable of making a shift, creating what is needed for themselves.

In the therapeutic world potency refers to the therapist being more powerful than the resistant forces of the internal Parent, who might obstruct change. In the client's head the Parent may speak with a voice of wrath. Steiner (1974: Chapter 21) wrote of protection and permission that enable the client to develop their own potency. This plays down the potency of the therapist.

Potency in the coaching context might be demonstrated by the coach working effectively and with credibility. The client can believe in and respect the coach. The coach can demonstrate their track record in making powerful interventions that have enabled change for their clients. The coach might show courage and assertiveness in offering what they notice in the client at any given moment. The coach may give feedback about language patterns, or vocal tone, gestures or movement. This offering of data enables the client to be more fully and consciously aware of what they are doing. This is a precursor to understanding, learning and then doing something differently.

(d) Working Styles

Taibi Kahler used Berne's five behaviour clues – words, tones, gestures, postures and facial expressions – while observing video-tapes for several weeks, with the result that he identified five defence-like behaviours that he called drivers after Freud's drive, or basic instinct, to repetitive behaviour. He went on to include the five drivers in the article about the miniscript (Kahler and Capers, 1974).

Hay (1989, 2009 [1992], 1997) introduced the term 'working style' as a label for the positive aspects of the drivers, commenting that: 'The TA concept of drivers provides an easy-to-use model of working styles that is readily recognised and applied in ways to suit different people. Based on original work by Taibi Kahler, it has been developed over the years into a relatively simple set of five characteristic styles. These were called drivers to reflect the "driven", or compulsive, quality of them when we are under stress. Identified first in therapy settings, the styles can still be recognised in somewhat less extreme forms in each of us. They are subconscious attempts by us to behave in ways that will gain us the recognition we need from others; they are also programmed responses to the messages we carry in our heads from important people in the past' (Hay, 2009 [1992]).

The five working styles are: Be Perfect, Be Strong, Please People, Try Hard and Hurry Up.

Each working style has positive assets that we use to stay 'OK':

- 'Be Perfect' is characterised by purposeful, high standards, attention to detail and preparedness.
- 'Be Strong' is focused on self-sufficiency, resilience and the determination to succeed.
- 'Please People' is a style that behaves generously to others, is polite, considerate and warm.
- 'Try Hard' is expressed through passionate interest, persistence and sympathy for the underdog.
- 'Hurry Up' works fast and achieves a lot in a short space of time, responding well to tight deadlines.

When the working styles are over-used, under stress, they result in compulsions that can de-rail and cause difficulty by increasing stressful behavioural patterns.

Each driver message has an antidote or 'allower'; this is also the work of Kahler and Capers (1974) Some of these may have come from your parents and you can also install them yourself, when you choose to do so.

Driver:	Allower:
Be Perfect	You're good enough as you are
Be Strong	Be open and express your wants
Please People	Please yourself
Try Hard	Do it
Hurry Up	Take your time

It is useful to be mindful in exploring these possibilities. Treading lightly and being respectful of feelings are important in any approach.

(e) *Psychological Distance*

When a coach works with a client in the context of an organisation, there is also a connection with the entity that represents that organisation. This may be the line manager, the human resources (HR) professional, the coach broker or the overall sponsor of a programme of work. In order for healthy 'OK' work to be done, there probably needs to be a contract in place, which accounts for the psychological needs of all three entities, as well as for the processes and practicalities.

When this contract is clear, explicit across all three parties and everyone understands the outcomes, measures and ways of working, it is likely that there is an equivalence of connection. This can be illustrated by an equilateral triangle, representing an appropriate professional set-up that is designed to avoid collusion of any two parties against the third.

Micholt (1992) wrote an influential article that described the imbalances and distortions that arise when there is collusion. The triangle in these circumstances loses its equitable structure and two points come closer together, pushing away the third. This may be described as follows:

1   The coach may side with the client against the corporate entity, in which case the coach is likely to be Rescuing. This happens when there is little involvement or communication from the organisation, which can lead to mistrust and resentment. In this case the coach may not respond appropriately to the client's need to find their voice and orientate more usefully.

2   The coach may be colluding with the organisation's representative. Goals may be set without reference to the client. The coach, in effect, takes on the organisation's agenda. The client then experiences the coach as Persecuting, and therefore feels isolated in the coaching process. This may lead to resistance and lack of engagement from the client.

3   The coach may feel excluded by the organisational figure who colludes with the client, for example in paying lip service to the commissioning of coaching. The coach is likely to adopt a more Victim mentality in this situation and feel disempowered and not respected. There may be a mismatch of values played out and this further exacerbates the situation.

If a coach takes their difficulty with psychological distance to a supervisor, it is important for the supervisor to be vigilant and not step into a collusive discussion with the coach. Otherwise, this would amplify the original difficulty. The supervisor is well advised, having spotted the distortion, to invite the coach to work out how to establish a healthier contract.

General

This section of themes and theories relates to more general frameworks, models and techniques, all of which have been written about extensively by originators and experts. As we have mentioned them in the book, we have summarised what we believe to be their essence; should you wish to read further on the topics, we have included some references in the Bibliography. You may choose to run an internet search by topic – you will be spoilt for choice.

(a)   Fundamental attribution error

'Ordinary moral thought often commits what social psychologists call, the fundamental attribution error. This is the error of ignoring situational factors and over confidently assuming that distinctive behaviours or patterns of behaviour are due to an agent's distinctive character trait. In fact, there is no evidence that people have character traits (virtues, vices, etc.) in the relevant sense. Since attribution of character traits leads to much evil, we should try to educate ourselves and others to stop doing it' (Harman, 1999: 315–331).

In the field of social psychology, this is also known as an 'attribution effect' or 'correspondence bias'. Jones and Harris (1967; see also Glasser and Salmon, 1995) conducted a survey in which participants were asked to read essays for and against Fidel Castro and rate the pro-Castro attitudes of the writers. Even when the participants were told that the writers' positions were determined by the toss of a coin, they still rated the writers as having a more positive attitude than the anti-Castro writers. They were unable to see the influence of the situational constraints put on the writers and take them into account when making their rating decisions.

Peppered through our stories are examples of fundamental attribution error. We can point to examples where we have 'taken positions' on situations that have not taken context and external factors into account. We also have examples of where we have taken this into account and done fabulous work with and for our clients, opening blind spots, inviting exploration of context and helping to reframe a situation.

Being aware of this phenomenon is crucial for a coach because it enables them to aid the client to re-frame, re-see, explore and view a situation from different perspectives, and can go a long way to freeing them from an unhelpful and often inaccurate place that is holding them back, derailing them or preventing them from seeing opportunities.

In our practices, we have developed a broad repertoire of tools and techniques to work with on this topic. These need not be complicated or sophisticated, for example simple stakeholder mapping, challenging assumptive phrases the client uses, asking questions about the broader context, which will all add value in some form.

In addition to being aware of this for your client, as a coach you must also be aware of your own fundamental attribution errors. Yet, this is challenging to do on your own. As the adage goes, the fish is the last one to see the sea. We have both chosen to take up one-to-one and group supervision throughout our coaching careers, and this topic is a good example of where having a second set of eyes (or several if working in a group) can be truly illuminating.

'Shoshin' is a term that originates from Zen Buddhism and means 'beginner's mind'. This relates to a state of mind that is open, eager and free from preconceptions when studying a subject. Many coaching books and training courses hold this as the key mind-set for coaches. Aspiring to hold and consciously maintaining a beginner's mind with each client will allow more into the coaching space for exploration and meaningful work.

As a final thought on the power of context, there have been many experiments on well-educated and 'respectable' people who have been profoundly affected by their context, stereotypes, roles and expectations of others than they could ever have believed. Milgram's classic experiment was set in the 1960s, in which people were invited to participate in a study into obedience of authority figures. The volunteers were known as 'teachers' and were responsible for administering shocks to a 'learner' when they answered a question incorrectly. Milgram polled senior year psychology majors to predict the behaviour of 100 hypothetical teachers. The responses ranged from 0/100 to 3/100 for those they thought would administer the maximum voltage. In the first set of experiments, 65% (26/40) administered the final 450-volt shock, despite hearing screams and requests to stop from the learner. The full details of the study are summarised in his 1973 article, 'The Perils of Obedience'.

Context is king.

(b) Chemistry

Before a coaching assignment starts, a coach and client will typically meet for a 'chemistry' session. As the name implies, this is a meeting to test the connection between the coach and client to ensure that both are comfortable and can form a useful and productive working relationship.

The nature of these sessions is varied. Some coaches will run a relatively formal session with an agenda to ensure that the criteria, which they consider important in building a solid coaching relationship, are in place. Other coaches will engage in an informal session that is more like grabbing a coffee for a chat. There is no right or wrong way to do a chemistry session, but it is considered good practice to have this step in place before either side commits to the coaching. It is an opportunity to build and test a contract, a mutually created verbal agreement, together.

It is important to note that the chemistry must work for both the coach and the client. Often clients initially think this is a one-way decision and overlook the fact that the coach also has choice and voice in the relationship. As coaching is a joint endeavour, it is important that both parties believe the relationship can work and chemistry sessions are a key step in making that happen.

(c)   Contracting

It is likely that every coach training programme will cover the importance of contracting in a coaching relationship. The contract sets out the scope and nature of the work and underpins the whole coaching process and professional connection.

Contracting will typically cover:

1   The commercial issues: what the work is, what the costs are, payment processes, early closure of the contract, handling postponements or cancellations, etc.
2   The logistical issues: where to meet, for how long, at what frequency, over what period of time, handling of data and note taking, etc.
3   The professional purpose: what the goals and outcomes are and how success will be measured, what is the primary focus of the intervention?
4   The psychological issues: confidentiality, including the reciprocal nature of this between coach and client, trust, balance of support and challenge, openness and disclosure, etc. The quality of the psychological contract will determine the overall effectiveness of coaching.

Determining these points is usually straightforward where only the paying client and coach are involved in the contracting. As more stakeholders are involved, the contracting process can become increasingly complex and sensitive. Where the paying client is the organisation or firm, there is another party to include in the contracting processes and they may well have different or conflicting needs. Where this is the case, it is imperative that the coach conducts clean and thorough contracting of the coaching work to ensure that no party is compromised or unclear on what the 'deal' is. This may include three-way conversations with the client and the line manager or coaching sponsor present.

Contracting well means that expectations are explicit and effectively managed. Disappointments are therefore more likely to be mitigated and successful outcomes achieved.

(d) Flow

Positive psychology has contributed significantly to the coaching field. One example of this is the research conducted by Mihaly Csikszentmihalyi on how to attain the state of peak performance, or as he calls it 'flow'.

Flow is often described as a state where one is utterly absorbed in an activity or situation to the extent that nothing else seems to matter, including time, ego and basic human needs like food.

Csikszentmihalyi's research identified several conditions that need to be in place for a flow-like state to be achieved including:

- Clear goals at every step
- Immediate feedback on actions
- A balance between skill and challenge
- Action and awareness become one – they merge
- Distractions are excluded from consciousness
- There is no fear of failure
- Self-consciousness disappears, there is no ego
- Time becomes distorted
- The activity becomes an end in itself.

Csikszentmihalyi concluded that there are some people who have developed their flow to such an extent that they are able to translate every potential threat into a pleasurable challenge and in doing so can maintain an inner tranquillity as a continuous state of mind; he called this state autotelic.

(e) Supervision Triangle incorporating parallel process

Eric Berne (1961: 83) talks about the hungers that all human beings experience. In Cochrane and Newton (2018: 55–64) they introduce the supervision triangle and explain its purpose and relevance.

The supervision triangle sets out three areas of attention, in supervision conversations, with a coach. Supervision is a conversation in relationship with a coach colleague, one where the coach wishes to reflect upon a specific topic from their coaching practice, with an experienced, wise and qualified supervisor. The supervision role involves the capability to take account of:

1. The coach's professional **management** of their coaching, the contract, the ethics, the process, the potential influence of sponsors, line managers and organisation cultures in the work
2. The coach's **development** as a coach and practitioner, their conscious awareness, learning and growth
3. The coach as a person, offering **support**, care and acknowledgment of the coach in their coaching context.

This approach is to ensure the supervisor is more agile, mindful and effective when working with a fellow coach, the supervisee.

In exploring an example of a supervision intervention, the concept of the positive parallel process is useful. 'Parallel process' is the term Searles (1955) called a 'reflection process'. In effect as supervisor, how might one role model positive and useful behaviours that enable the coach to make a different choice with their client? This has the potential, via the coach, to flow back into the client's world and make a positive shift in their wider system or organisation.

Consider this example: a coach arrives in supervision with concerns about chaotic behaviours from the client. This chaos may show up in the demeanour of the coach, who may arrive late, expressing that they haven't had time to clarify their supervision question and that they're sorry they had to rearrange. The coach may describe their client as being haphazard, not confirming dates and arrangements, and being unsure what they want to work on. On examination the coach might notice that their own behaviours mirror the client's workplace culture and that as coach they have taken this on inadvertently.

Intervention: it is important that the supervisor behaves with clarity and consistency throughout the conversation. A specific mutual contract discussed during the supervision conversation is powerful. The coach also needs to feel supported by the supervisor to understand the impact of the chaotic behaviours on their own well-being and confidence. The coach can find a healthier way forward for themselves. The coach develops insight about what stimulated this chaotic behaviour in them.

Refining their coaching approach with this client in the future stems from the beneficial learning. The coach decides what they would like to do differently next time.

Impact: the coach then behaves more usefully with their client, holding boundaries and contracting effectively; this models new possibilities for the client who may also shift more in this direction.

Potentially the client interacts differently with colleagues as a consequence of the coach's behavioural modelling. The client can be clearer with others about what is wanted, and by when.

Being a more confident and grounded coach in future sessions has implications for wider coaching practice with other clients and contexts. The supervisor is also learning with the supervisee, the supervisor honouring their needs, which are evident in co-creating the relationship.

(f) The GROW model

The GROW model is undoubtedly one of the most commonly known and used coaching frameworks in the world. It was developed by the late Sir John Whitmore (2002) and is published in his book, *Coaching for Performance: GROWing People, Performance and Purpose.*

The model is both simple and complex in that it is easy to understand and follow on a practical level, yet there is depth to the model that more experienced coaching practitioners can access and apply.

The model provides a structure to follow in a coaching session. This structure can apply equally to a 15-minute coaching conversation as to a 2-hour-long conversation.

The coaching conversation starts with 'G', which is the goal. The coach asks questions to establish both the overall goal(s) for the coaching assignment as well as the goal for the specific session.

Once clear, the coaching conversation can move to 'R', which is reality. This step in the model is intended to establish the reality in which the goal exists, i.e. what are the context, the facts, the assumptions and the data relating to the goal the client wants to work on? In establishing the map of the territory, the client will have all the information related to the goal in front of them and so will have a full picture to work from rather than a filtered one.

The 'O', or options, step of the model is intended to enable the client to create possible options in volume. This step is about generating options in quantity; it is not necessarily about finding the solution. The options generated need not be feasible solutions in their current state and this is typical; the idea at this stage is to expand the number of possible options to allow new ideas to develop before narrowing down the options to feasible solutions or actions.

The final step 'W' is focused on will. There are two parts to this: first what the client will now do, i.e. what actions will they take? Second, how motivated the client is to follow through. In order for the coaching to have effect, there needs to be clear action(s) and a willingness to make it happen.

(g)   Competencies

Professional coaching bodies have put a huge amount of effort into developing comprehensive coaching competencies alongside codes of conduct. These offer a way of 'doing' coaching and each professional coaching body requires, or at the very least encourages, its members to engage in a programme of ongoing continuous professional development.

Enhancing your skills and competence as a coach is important and we would wholeheartedly advocate that all coaches engage with a progressive journey of learning and development in order to be the best coach they can be and to best serve their clients' needs.

In addition to developing technical coaching capability, our experience tells us that coaches also need to pay good attention to their way of 'being' and, in doing so, we believe that coaches will not only deliver great coaching but they will be great coaches too.

Bibliography

Berne, E. (1961) *Transactional Analysis in Psychotherapy: A Systemic and Social Psychiatry*. New York: Grove Press.

Berne, E. (1966) *Games People Play: The Psychology of Human Relationships*. London: Penguin Life.

Berne, E. (1973) *What Do You Say After Hello?* New York: Grove Press.

Broadwell, M. J. (1969) 'Teaching For Learning (XVI)'. *The Gospel Guardian* 20(41): 1–3a.

Choy, A. (1990) 'The Winners' Triangle.' *Transactional Analysis Journal*, 20: 40–46.

Cochrane, H. and Newton, T. (2011) *Supervision for Coaches: A Guide to Thoughtful Work*. Ipswich: Supervision for Coaches Publishing.

Cochrane, H. and Newton, T. (2018) *Supervision and Coaching: Growth and Learning in Professional Practice*. Abingdon, New York: Routledge.

Crossman, P. (1966) 'Permission and Protection.' *Transactional Analysis Bulletin*, 5(19): 152–154.

Csikszentmihalyi, M. (1990) *Flow: The Psychology of Optimal Experience*. New York: Harper & Row.

Csikszentmihalyi, M. (1997) *Finding Flow*. New York: Basic Books.

De Bono, E. (1985) *Six Thinking Hats*. Toronto: Key Porter Books Ltd.

Doran, G. T. (1981) 'There's a S.M.A.R.T. Way to Write Managements' Goals and Objectives.' *Management Review*, 70: 35–36.

Dörnyei, Z. (2001) *Motivational Strategies in the Language Classroom*. Cambridge: Cambridge Language Teaching Library.

Ernst, F. (1971) 'The OK Corral: The Grid for Get-on-with.' *Transactional Analysis Journal*, 1(4): 231–240

Glasser, T. and Salmon, C. T. (1995) *Public Opinion and the Commissioning of Consent*. New York: The Guilford Press.

Harman, G. (1999) 'Moral Philosophy Meets Social Psychology: Virtue Ethics and the Fundamental Attribution Error.' *Proceedings of Aristotelian Society New Series*, 99: 315–331.

Hay, J. (1997) 'Transformational Mentoring: Using Transactional Analysis to Make a Difference.' *Transactional Analysis Journal*, 27(3): 158–167.

Hay, J. (2009) *Transactional Analysis for Trainers*, 2nd edn. Broadoak End, Hertford: Sherwood Publishing [1st edn 1992].

Hay, J. and Williams, N. (1989) 'The Reluctant Time Manager.' *Opportunities* May.

Jones, E. E. and Harris, V.A. (1967) 'The Attribution of Attitudes.' *Journal of Experimental Social Psychology*, 3(1): 1–24.

Kahler, T. (1975) 'Drivers: The Key to the Process of Scripts.' *Transactional Analysis Journal*, 5(3): 280–284.

Kahler, T. and Capers, H. (1974) 'The Miniscript.' *Transactional Analysis Journal*, 4(1): 26–42.

Karpman, S. (1968) 'Fairy Tales and Script Drama Analysis.' *Transactional Analysis Bulletin*, 7(26): 39–43.

Micholt, N. (1992) 'Psychological Distance and Group Interventions.' *Transactional Analysis Journal*, 22: 228–233.

Milgram, S. (1973) 'The Perils of Obedience.' *Harper's Magazine*, 62–77.

Napper, R. and Newton, T. (2000) *TACTICS: Transactional Analysis Concepts for All Trainers, Teachers and Tutors + Insight into Collaborative Learning Strategies*. Ipswich: The Riverside Press.

Peter, T.J. and Waterman Jnr, R.H. (2006) *In Search of Excellence*. New York: Harper Collins.

Searles, H. (1955) 'The Informational Value of the Supervisor's Emotional Experience.' In: *Collected Papers on Schizophrenia and Related Subjects*. London: Hogarth Press.

Steiner, C. (1974) *Scripts People Live: Transactional Analysis of Life Scripts*. New York: Grove Press.

Stewart, I. and Joines, V. (1987) *TA Today: A New Introduction to Transactional Analysis*. Nottingham, NC: Lifespace Publishing.

Whitmore, J. (2002) *Coaching for Performance GROWing People, Performance and Purpose*. London: Nicholas Brealey Publishing.

me:my™coach

Having witnessed the unfolding coaching stories of 'flowing and falling', you might like to explore your own coaching practice further.

Karen Dean has developed an online framework called me:my™coach in support of continuing professional development for coaches. Go to www.memycoach.com.

Here you can examine your coaching conversations, track your progress, and explore what you missed and what you did well. Develop your own solutions to improve your subsequent client interventions. Determine and commit to actions. Gather quality data about your work, noticing themes, increasing awareness as you grow as a coach.

This is also an excellent way of preparing well for a supervision conversation, deriving best value.

me:my™coach is a cost-effective investment in your coaching skills, with this original comprehensive online tool: 'Digital Technology with Emotional Intelligence.'

Index

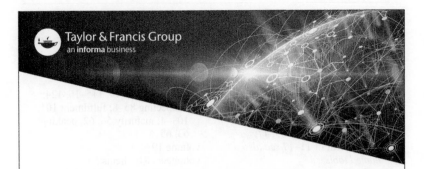